Propagandaman

A superhero for the inverted Fascist state

By Steve Spears

ISBN: 0692314040 / 9780692314043

Library of Congress Control Number:
2014918657
Mussopo Publishing, River Forest, IL
United States

"Convictions are more dangerous foes of truth than lies."

— Nietzsche

This book is dedicated to all who are skeptical of convictions.

This book could not have been written without the centuries of prolific determination, by those who have a low tolerance for b.s., even when they are the source.

Chapter one

Deep in the bowels of the Phiz-bang pharmaceuticals research laboratories, high security, secret sub-basement, there is a brilliant young scientist on the verge of a revolutionary breakthrough in copy-cat drug patent manipulation. His name is Sam Hyam and he has been working tirelessly and alone for the past seven years to design and build a machine that can analyze the chemical composition of wildly profitable drugs and automatically generate new versions of the same thing so that Phiz-bang pharmaceutical company can quadruple their profits by never having to fund research again.

Sam: "This is it. Just one more line of code and the Replicator 5000 will be ready for a test run." He wipes his forehead then taps out the machine code quickly and skillfully. Then pushing himself away from the desk, he zips around to one end of the elaborate machine, takes a little blue pill from a vial, and places it gently on a conveyor belt. His hand reaches for a big red button and with the feeling of anticipation rushing through his arm, he pushes the button.

The machine whirrs and crackles as the little blue pill moves into the mouth of the machine. The pill gets irradiated with laser beams, crushed through a grinder, blasted with strange vapors, and fired into a spinning chamber until vortical. Ten minutes later, the machine falls silent and Sam, waiting on the other side of his machine, looks concerned. A moment passes and then down a long translucent tube rolls a little blue pill onto the receiving tray. **Sam:** "Aahh, so far, so good, now I'll just check the re-invented formula to make sure it is market ready." He then sits in front of the computer screen and analyzes the new data, speaking out loud to himself about the chemical formula. "Amazing," He says. "So close, yet so... close. Tonight you will get a test run, my little blue friend." With that he slips the pill into a small plastic bag, puts it in his shirt pocket, and walks over to the elevator which will bring him to the ground level for a long over-due lunch.

Standing in the line of the spacious and modern cafeteria, Sam chooses his favorite, scallops with fettuccini alfredo and a large iced tea, then wanders over to a place near the window. It was nice, he thinks, to be able to see the outside world, after spending so many hours in his lab. All of the tables are taken except for one and Sam smiles as if it is one more sign of good fortune for his already monumentally fortunate day. He sits quietly, enjoying his lunch and gazing out the window with an expression of well earned, bliss.

Before he is five minutes into his meal, a man in a security guard uniform walks up and asks if he can sit with him. There is something in the man's voice that makes him uncomfortable but he is disinclined to be rude. He hesitates because he was really enjoying this moment of reverie but then thinks it might be good for him to socialize a little after such a great endeavor. "O.k., sure, have a seat." He says.

Guard: "Thank you, this is my favorite table. I sit here every day at this time. How come I have never seen you before? I thought I knew everyone. Are you new here?

Sam: (feeling that social discomfort again) "I work in R and D."

Guard: "Really, do you know Charlie Harris? He's a great guy; or how about Shelly Allen? Wow, what a babe! Man, I'd like to read her some Miranda rights, if you know what I mean."

Sam: (Pausing politely) "I don't believe we've met."

Guard: "I thought you worked in R and D. How can you not know who these people are, if you work in R and D?"

Sam: "I work by myself."

Guard: (Incredulously) "Really, what floor?"

Sam: "It's one of the lower levels."

Guard: "O.k., buddy, whatever. I'm just curious because I work security, swing shifts, and I've never seen you before. If you're in you're in and it's none of my business."

Sam takes another bite with some trepidation as if he was regretting the choice to go to the cafeteria. As he is chewing he looks across the table and notices the book the security guard has next to his tray. There's a picture of a round faced man with short hair and the title is, "Real America" by Ben Gleck. The stranger notices him noticing the book and launches into a synopsis.

Guard: "It's a book about how the liberals are trying to take over America with their liberal agenda, just like Hitler did with Nazi Germany and how we have to rise up together as Americans to stop them before it's too late and they ship our children off to re-education camps."

Sam: "Do you honestly believe that a totalitarian regime which brought devastation and genocide to Europe is equivalent to a political party that advocates for tolerance and assistance to the poor?"

Guard: "That is where it starts. First they tell you they want to do only good things and then when the masses are lulled and hypnotized by their goodness, then the daggers come out and they take away all of our freedoms. Look, you have to read the book. I can't explain it as well as he can. I'll let you borrow this copy, if you want. I have others I can read. You should read it. It will open your eyes!"

Sam: "Well I'd like to but, this project I have been working on has been taking up a lot of my time and (He gets up from the table) maybe I'll see you around here again and when things slow down for me (He picks up his tray and gets ready to start walking) you can lend it to me then."

Guard: "Are you sure? I don't need to

have it back right away."

Sam: "I'm sorry but (Looking at his watch) I really do have to go. I'm already late for my presentation. It was nice meeting you. Good bye now."

Sam turns and begins walking before the security guard could get the next word out. His eyes roll so hard he almost feels disoriented.

"Good bye and God bless America." The security guard says with unrivaled enthusiasm as Sam was moving with alacrity towards the elevator. The security guard watches as the elevator doors close and then something occurs to him, he slaps his forehead and says out loud to himself, "I could just go to the public library and check out another copy since I'm almost finished with it anyhow." So he looks to see where the elevator is going and he determines to go down there later and just drop it off as a gift.

Sam sits down at his desk and finishes his lunch in peace, then pulls the little plastic bag from his pocket.

Holding it up, he smiles once again and gets out his cell phone. His girlfriend, Leslie, answers: "Hello, it's about time you called me."

Sam: "I'm sorry. you know how I get lost in my work. Sometimes I don't even know what day it is."

Leslie: "Well, it's Tuesday and it's been four days since the last time I heard from you. For what do I deserve this honor?"

Sam: "Things are about to get really interesting around here."

Leslie: "And by interesting you mean... they're gonna finally drop your sorry butt?"

Sam: "I almost think you're losing faith in me."

Leslie: "You know exactly what I think and it's all good. So, what do you have in store for me?"

Sam: "Why don't I stop by tonight and I'll show you."

Leslie: "What, all show me and no tell me?"

Sam: "You will get plenty of both,

tonight."

Leslie: "It's not like you, to be mischievous. This must be what I think it is."

Sam: "I promise you, this is big news. So, how's about I pick you up at seven and we'll go to Café Olé."

Leslie: "Ooh, I love that place… Are you getting a promotion?"

Meanwhile, the security guard travels down the elevator to this level and wanders around until he finally finds the only room that looks like a laboratory. He can hear Sam's voice and he notices that he is walking into the middle of an intimate conversation, so he, tip-toes over to the closest place where he can set the book down. He leaves the book on the end of the conveyor and steps away quietly.

The conversation continues.

Sam: "Let me just say this… Buy stock in Phiz-bang, tomorrow."

Leslie: "If I can scrounge up enough money for a share, I might do that."

Sam: "I'll see you later."

Leslie: "See you, sugar."

Sam switches off his phone and tosses it on the desk. He leans back, smiling, kicks his feet up and folds his fingers behind his head. As he gets comfortable, however, he fails to notice how close his elbow is to the start button on his machine and does not turn around quick enough to notice that the book was being fed into it.

He hears something unusual in the processing stage and looks over on the monitor to see a strange display of the analysis, as the computer is struggling with the content. He couldn't understand what was happening. There shouldn't be anything on the display, he thinks, but he sees chains of molecules like he has never seen before. He is just about to hit the kill switch, but then decides to wait it out. A few moments later the machine becomes silent and Sam watches as a little crimson pill comes tumbling down the chute.

He looks at it for a long time, as if

he were witnessing a ghost. He stands back from the machine and speaks to it, "Are you alive in there, Franken-computer? Who taught you how to do that? It sure wasn't me." He holds the pill close to his eyes, at a loss to explain his sudden urge to personify his creation. He returns to the computer to look again for clues, something that might point him in the right direction.

A few hours go by and still he feels that he is no closer to making sense of it. He looks at his watch. "I've gotta get out of here before I start hallucinating." He then put's the pill in another plastic bag, holds it up again, and shakes it saying, "Are you a daemon seed? ...Looking for a place to spawn? Maybe I should grind you up and sprinkle you over the circuitry of my X-phone, just for kicks." Then he puts it in his pocket.

As he leaves the building he's in a daze with ideas. He babbles to himself incoherently as he drives, randomly, rattling off the things he had seen on the computer screen, "That combination… somewhere a number dropped… maybe too much compression… couldn't be materials." Suddenly he finds himself parked in front of Leslie's apartment building and realizes that he didn't even notice that he was driving. He gets out and shakes his head to try and stay focused on where he is. "I've got to get my mind off of this problem or this evening will go down like the Hindenburg." He walks up a flight of stairs quickly and rings the bell.

The door opens and the, smiling, Leslie greets him enthusiastically. "How's my mad scientist?" She's wearing a chartreuse dress, with matching fabric flowers on one shoulder.

Sam: "Much better now. It's good to see you. You look… (He embraced her and kissed her softly.) …Like a teacher I once had a crush on."

Leslie: "I'm still a teacher."

Sam: "And I still have that crush."

Leslie: "So, how's it going?"
Sam: "It's just … been a weird and exciting, unusually bizarre, day." She seems puzzled by the odd sentence and he is aware of how it must sound.
Sam: "Let's go I'll tell you on the way." As they walk towards the car, he still has that faraway look. Then in the car, he put the key in the ignition, but hesitated for several seconds before turning it.
Leslie: "Huston to Sam, it is time to return from orbit."
Sam: "Sorry, it's just that I saw… well, I don't know what I saw and that's what's bugging me…"
Leslie: "Do you want me to drive?"
Sam: "Do you mind."
Leslie: "If you're going to start ranting about things like Schrodinger's cat and the collapsing of realities, it would probably be better to let me pilot the terra-craft."
Sam: "Yeah you're right. I'm surprised I even made it here." They switch places and Sam begins to

explain what happened.

Sam: "I thought I had the project completed and even did a successful test run."

Leslie: "Congratulations, that's fantastic!"

Sam: "Thank you. Yes it is, and a great relief, because there were a few times when I didn't think it was going anywhere. But, after I got off the phone with you... No, wait, let me back up. I took a break... and got some lunch and then I called you... and after I got off the phone, I was leaning back in my chair when my elbow accidentally hit the start button and my computer screen lit up like a casino."

Leslie: "Just from touching one button?"

Sam: "Well, usually, that is perfectly normal, but I didn't recognize anything I was looking at."

Leslie: "Garbage in garbage out, right? The computer can only follow the directions it is given. So, are you blaming yourself?"

Sam: "No, actually I am questioning my sanity… Anyhow, this stuff shows up on the computer screen and I can't make any sense of it and then ten minutes later a pill shows up at the other end. I was sure there was nothing going through there, but it was like the thing had a mind of its own.

Leslie: "Maybe you should try to do a dry run, tomorrow, see if it happens again."

Sam: "Yeah, I'll try that, but it shouldn't make it difference. It's not programmed that way."

Leslie: "I'm sure you'll figure it out."

Sam: "I'm sure, you're sure."

Leslie: "I'm sure, you're sure, I'm sure."

Sam: "I think you're onto something."

Leslie: …"Sure."

Later on they are at the restaurant, enjoying themselves and escaping into the mundane. Leslie is telling him a story about someone from her job as a school teacher.

Leslie: "So, this little girl, I will call

her 'Natasha', shows up with her science project and it's a flow chart, pun intended, of the menstrual cycle." (laughing)

Sam: "How old is she?"

Leslie: "This is fourth grade. She's nine years old!"

Sam: "Apparently, her mother doesn't want to leave these matters to the school board."

Leslie: "I know, but it was adorable to see the look of clinical seriousness on her face, in spite of all the snickering of the boys."

Sam: "Were there, detailed illustrations?"

Leslie: "Oohh yess, (laughing) and props."

Sam: "So, Mom is a Gynecologist, eh?"

Leslie: "No, but she practices some kind of medicine. I forget what it is."

Sam: "Speaking of Gynecology, do you require some dessert?"

Leslie: "I'm not quite there, yet, but I could go for some preliminary chocolate, like this flourless Godiva cake with raspberries. Do you think you might like a bite?"

Sam: "Are they forbidden raspberries?"

Leslie: "Actually, these ones, it says here, will bring you back in to the garden of earthly delights."

Sam: "Let's go… I'm just gonna go tackle the waiter (Sam feigns getting up)."

They order the dessert and later head back to her apartment.

Leslie: "Would you like to come in for a cup of coffee?" (She says with an exaggerated Lauren Bacall, voice).

Sam: "Do you have any sugar? I need lots of sugar."

Leslie: "I got all the sugar you want, baby."

Steaminess ensues and after a round or two of romantic gymnastics, Sam decides to try out the copy-cat blue pill. He reaches into his shirt pocket, which is on the floor, and feeling for it, pops it into his mouth. They return to lovemaking but, the pill never seems to take effect.

Sam: "I don't think anything is happening."

Leslie: "Are you sure?"

Sam: "Oh, no!" He jumps up to turn the light on and sees the little plastic bag with the blue pill next to his shirt on the floor. "Oh, sh*t. This is not good."

Leslie: "You took the other one by mistake?"

Sam: (With a grave expression) "Yes."

Leslie: "Maybe we should go to the emergency room."

Sam: "But nothing happened to me, and that was at least forty minutes ago. There would be nothing they could do for me."

Leslie: "They could at least monitor you, in case something does start to happen."

Sam: "What am I going to say, 'I accidentally took a pill for which I have no prescription and no one does, because the drug has not been invented yet.' Then I have to launch into an explanation of what I have been working on for the past seven years, but it's top secret and only I know about it... They will have me in an asylum or prison by sunrise."

Leslie: "Maybe you could try to purge what's left of it."

Sam: "I doubt it would do much good. Too much time has passed."

Leslie: "Then come lie down with me and I'll try to help you relax."

Sam: (Reluctantly) "O.k."

With a worried look on his face, Sam tries to rest. The light is off but Sam cannot sleep. He gets up and slips out in the middle of the night and starts wandering the streets. Some time passes and he finds himself near a park where several people have been camped out in protest of Wall Street's manipulation of the political system. A policeman stops him before he can pass."

Cop: "You better get outta here. Things are about to get ugly."

Sam: "What do you mean?"

Cop: "We have a job to do and lots of tear gas and pepper spray is gonna get used."

Sam: "Don't they have a constitutional right to assemble? You know… the first amendment?"

Cop: "I am not going to argue with you, that is not my job. Now I suggest you move along."

Sam: "Don't you care about what the constitution means for our representative democracy?"

Cop: "The mayor doesn't like it. He says it looks bad. Now we have a job to do, don't we?"

Another policeman on a horse rides up and says, "Is this guy given you trouble?" (To the cop).

Cop 1: "No, he was just leaving."

Cop 2: (Pokes Sam with a baton) "You heard what the officer said. Go get a job or move back home with your parents."

Sam: "I was just walking by. I'm not with them."

Cop 2: "Well, go walk by somewhere else."

Sam looks out at the field of tents that are about to get raided and suddenly feels a mysterious sensation pulsing through him. People are starting to come out of their tents and they know what's about to happen. Flashes of media imagery blaze through his consciousness. He is confused and overwhelmed. Then for some bizarre reason he speaks out and his voice booms with the power of ten megaphones: "PROTESTING DOES NOT ACCOMPLISH ANYTHING! HISTORY HAS SHOWN THAT YOU ARE BETTER OFF STAYING HOME AND WATCHING TELEVISION!!

The policemen are startled by the incredible volume of his voice and step back as if they are witnessing something supernatural.

Sam: (Repeating) "PROTESTING DOES NOT ACCOMPLISH ANYTHING! HISTORY HAS SHOWN THAT YOU ARE BETTER

OFF STAYING HOME AND WATCHING TELEVISION!!

Sam looks resolute, as if the powerful words erupting from his authoritative lungs carry a truth which is heavier than the mountains: "PROTESTING DOES NOT ACCOMPLISH ANYTHING! HISTORY HAS SHOWN THAT YOU ARE BETTER OFF STAYING HOME AND WATCHING TELEVISION!!

Protesters are emerging quickly from their tents and they stare at this strange man as if they are in a trance.
Sam: "PROTESTING DOES NOT ACCOMPLISH ANYTHING! HISTORY HAS SHOWN THAT YOU ARE BETTER OFF STAYING HOME AND WATCHING TELEVISION!!

The police are all looking at Sam with astonishment because they see that his absurd message is having a real affect.
Sam: "PROTESTING DOES NOT ACCOMPLISH ANYTHING! HISTORY HAS SHOWN THAT YOU

ARE BETTER OFF STAYING HOME AND WATCHING TELEVISION!!

Gradually the protesters begin breaking down their tents and folding them up.

Sam: "PROTESTING DOES NOT ACCOMPLISH ANYTHING! HISTORY HAS SHOWN THAT YOU ARE BETTER OFF STAYING HOME AND WATCHING TELEVISION!!

The police are beginning to smile and nudge each other and make comments. It is too much for them to believe.

Sam: "PROTESTING DOES NOT ACCOMPLISH ANYTHING! HISTORY HAS SHOWN THAT YOU ARE BETTER OFF STAYING HOME AND WATCHING TELEVISION!!

The protesters, in zombie like fashion pack up all of their equipment, along with their trash and begin to disperse.

Sam: "PROTESTING DOES NOT ACCOMPLISH ANYTHING! HISTORY HAS SHOWN THAT YOU

ARE BETTER OFF STAYING HOME
AND WATCHING TELEVISION!!
Cop 1: It's working! I don't freakin
believe it. It's working.
Sam: "PROTESTING DOES NOT
ACCOMPLISH ANYTHING!
HISTORY HAS SHOWN THAT YOU
ARE BETTER OFF STAYING HOME
AND WATCHING TELEVISION!!

With all of the protesters scattering
away, the officer on the horse says,
"What did you do? How did you make
that happen? I've never seen anything
like that!"
Sam: "I am the new opiate of the
masses." (Then he walks away with a
confident and indignant, stride).
Cop 1: "Hey buddy, what's your
name!?"

Sam does not respond. He just
keeps on walking.

Chapter Two

Sam wakes up on the floor of his apartment. Not remembering what happened or how he got there. The phone begins ringing and he fumbles through his jacket to find it.

Sam: "Hi, I'm sorry I didn't stay. I couldn't sleep and needed to go for a walk."

Leslie: "Turn on your television, Hurry."

Sam: "What is it? What channel?" Sam reaches for the remote.

Leslie: "I think it's you. On channel nine, or five, or three. It looks like they're all running the story."

Sam: "Me? …What about Me."

Leslie: "I don't know. It looks like you. The video isn't too clear."

Sam finds the channel.

News announcer: "Sources say that this man, the one you see in the bottom, right side of your screen, spoke to the swarm of protesters who had been camped out at Talinni Park for fifteen days, in a voice that was, quote, "As loud as thunder and as hypnotizing as Rasputin's." end quote." In as little as twelve minutes, the protesters packed all of their belongings, cleaned up the park, and left quietly. The police had been planning a raid on the park, but then called it off for obvious reasons. We still don't know the identity of the man in question, but this station is posting a reward for anyone who can provide us with information as to the identity of this mysterious man."

Leslie: "That's you, isn't it?"

Sam: "I don't know; it looks like me. It kinda sounds like me, but the sound is so distorted, I can't even make out what is being said… This is weird. I don't remember what happened after I left your place last night, really."

Leslie: "Do you remember leaving your car here?"

Sam: "I remember that I went for a walk."

Leslie: "Do you remember the great time we had last night?"

Sam: "Yeah, tremendous, up until the part where I freaked out because of that mystery pill."

Leslie: "How are you feeling now?"

Sam: "O.K., I guess, except I don't how I got home. But that's not unusual for me."

Leslie: "I'm sorry."

Sam: "Oh yes, it was your fault. You were the femme fatale. I was ensnared by your hypnotic charms."

Leslie: "O.k., you can stop now."

Sam: "You were divine, like Aphrodite, Lilith, and Mata Hari, all rolled into one. My head was in the clouds, obviously. Still kinda is."

Leslie: "Aren't you supposed to be at the lab now?"

Sam: "I have a long leash.. If I call and give them good news, they'll be more than happy to let me take a break. Besides, I want to see if I can find out more about what happened last night. This is like the Twilight Zone."

Leslie: "Well, I'm gonna be late myself if I don't get it in gear, so I'll talk to you later O.k. Call me when you figure it out."

Sam: "Sure enough. I'll see ya."

Leslie: "Bye, Honey."

Sam returns to watching television and now they are showing a field reporter interviewing a police officer.

Cop: "It was unbelievable. This guy just kept repeating something like, 'Protesting doesn't work and history shows you gotta go get a job if you wanna watch TV.' And he just kept saying it over and over and over and it just seemed to keep getting louder and louder. We had to cover our ears. And before you knew it, the protesters were gone. It sure made our jobs easier. If you ask me, that guy is a real American hero."

Reporter: "There you have it from Officer Finnegan of the 32nd precinct; Back to you Michelle."

Then the news switches to sports and Sam turns off the set. After a few moments in thought, he decides to look for a psychologist on the internet.

Eventually he goes to the university nearby to talk to someone there, because he can't get an appointment, and doesn't really feel the need for it. Besides, he has friends at the university who can just make a phone call.

Sam takes a cab over to where his car was parked and then goes to visit an old chemistry professor who refers him to a Dr. Bradlebaum, a specialist in neuropsychology. Sam then walks across campus and stands in his office doorway.

Sam: "Hi, Dr. Lawrence suggested that I talk to you. I know you are probably quite busy, so I'll be quick. There was a man on the news this morning and I have reason to believe it was me, but I have no memory of the event. I don't think that I have a mental health issue, but I want to be cautious."

Dr. Bradlebaum: (Speaking with a heavy accent) "So you are the propaganda man."

Sam: "What do you mean?"

Dr. Bradlebaum: "Make the lie big,

make it simple, keep telling it and eventually the people will believe it. This is the developed technique of Joseph Goebbels, the Minister of propaganda for the Third Reich. "People will more readily fall victims to the big lie than the small lie, since they themselves often tell small lies in little matters but would be ashamed to resort to large-scale falsehoods. It would never come into their heads to fabricate colossal untruths, and they would not believe that others could have the impudence to distort the truth so infamously."

Sam: "That sounds familiar. But if it was me, and I have no memory of it, what would account for such a thing?"

Dr. Bradlebaum: "Dissociative amnesia, brought about by disease or injury of the brain and/or severe emotional trauma. However, I am not a therapist. If you wish, I could give you the telephone number for someone who could better help you."

Sam: "Yes, thank you. I need to do

something to resolve this."

Dr. B gives Sam a piece of paper with a name he found in his rolodex. Sam puts the piece of paper with the number in his pocket, says good bye to the professor and heads over to the library for a little research. It was now his deep concern that the pill he took the last night was what did the damage.

A couple hours later, as he is walking back to his car, he hears the cheering of a crowd behind him and a man with no clothing on, goes streaking past him, almost knocking him over in the process.

Sam: "YOUNG MAN! (The streaker stopped in astonishment at the sound of Sam's voice.) BEHOLD THE SOCIAL ENVIRONMENT IN WHICH YOU HAVE CHOSEN TO SHAME YOURSELF! WE HAVE ALL AGREED THAT CLOTHING IS GOOD FOR SOCIETY! NOW BY DISPLAYING YOURSELF SO, YOU ARE SAYING THAT EVERYONE IS WRONG EXCEPT FOR YOU!" The crowd of people begins to gather around and Sam begins to take on an almost super human stature. "IF YOU WISH TO BE TRULY NAKED, YOU MUST CLOTHE YOURSELF IN THE GOOD OPINION OF SOCIETY! IF YOU DO NOT EMBRACE THE FASHIONS OF YOUR GENERATION THEN YOU WILL BE CONDEMNED TO WANDER THE DESERTS OF INDIVIDUALITY AND SO-CALLED, FREE THOUGHT!"

Just then, campus security shows up and Tasers the nude man, causing him to collapse on the sidewalk. They then flip him over, zip cuff his wrists, and haul him away. Someone in the crowd puts two and two together and says, "Hey you're that guy from Talinni Park." Sam walks quickly away. Again the person in the crowd speaks, "That's the guy who dispersed the protesters at Talinni Park last night!" Sam is long gone before anyone thinks of following him.

Four hours later, Sam finds himself, lying on a bench, in a bus terminal with no memory of what had just transpired. He is confused and worries out loud about what was happening to him.

Sam: "Oh, my God, I am falling apart... It's like a bad dream that keeps looping? Think... Think." Then he hears a voice.

Voice: "Just do what I do." Sam turns to see a giddy, old Vagabond man on the bench next to him, hoisting a paper bag and singing. "When I'm all alone and blue as can be, drink a little drink with me."

Sam: "Can I ask you a personal question?"

Vagabond: "Only if it's a question with personality." (He chuckles).

Sam: "Do you believe in... fate... or is it all just.., whatever happens.., happens?

Vagabond: "Well.., you know what the king said?"

Sam: "You mean, the king of... England?"

Vagabond: "Ha! Yes, the king of England! Old King William. He said.., He said.., "Life is but a walking shadow…, a poor player who struts and frets his hour upon the stage and then is heard no more… It is a tale, told by an idiot, full of sound and fury.., signifying….. nothing."

Sam: "Thank you. That is exactly what I needed to hear." He says with some sarcasm.

Sam gets up, gives the man some money and begins moving again. Out on the street he reaches into his pocket and ferrets out the piece of paper he got from Dr. Bradlebaum. He puts it away and then after taking a few more steps, pulls it out again and dials the number. He gets the voice-mail.

"Hello, this is Dr. Soren's office. I am either in session or away from my desk. Please leave a detailed message, and I will return your call as soon as I am able; Beep."

Sam: "Hi, uh.., this is Sam. Sam Hyam. I got your number from a professor at I.O. University, named Bradlebaum. It's kind of… I need to talk to you. I mean, I would like to schedule a meeting at your earliest convenience. It's really..., well.., strange and anyhow if you have any cancellations, please call me. The number is: 777-555-1234. Thank you." He puts the phone away and looks up at the sky, anxiously.

Later that afternoon, as he is lying on the sofa and flipping through the channels, trying to find out more about what happened. The coverage is repetitive, so he decides to watch something else to relax and flipping through the channels some more, he comes upon a documentary about penguins.

He finds it pleasantly distracting, watching the way they waddle and huddle and mate. Sam slowly drifts away into sleep and begins to have a dream. In his dream he is walking through a field of tall corn at night. The moon is brighter than he has ever seen it. The glow is so powerful and rich, that it pulls at him. It tempers his breathing and tingles on his skin. The corn is planted in the form of a maze, circular in design. His inner dream voice whispers, "How odd, a maze of maize." Somehow, he instinctively moves toward the center.

After walking for a while he comes to a clearing. In the center of the clearing stand four men. Men who loom from beyond the grave, inspiring the imagination like no others. They are, Elvis Presley, Ronald Reagan, John Wayne, and Jerry Falwell. They stand like statues, watching Sam's approach. Elvis says, "Hey man, I'm all shook up about that crazy stuff you've been doing. You're like a hunk of burnnin love."

Sam: "I don't understand; why am I, here. What is happening to me?"

Ronald Reagan: "My fellow American, there comes a time in course of human events when those who would perpetrate evil against those who desire freedom, must be stopped by any means necessary, to preserve the shining city on the hill; the beacon of freedom which has been handed down to us by our forefathers and preserved in the sacred words of our constitution."

Sam: "Are you saying that I am supposed to fight the forces of evil? Are you sure you have the right guy? Have you seen my resume?"

John Wayne: "That's right partner. You're gonna ride into town, with both guns blazin, and bring some law and order. Just like ol' Duke used to do. And when you see the whites of their eyes, you just give em a taste of justice, western style."

Sam: "You want me to kill someone, hypothetically…, metaphorically? I am a scientist. I spend most of my time in laboratories and my face buried in books. This is a very weird career change you are proposing."

Jerry Falwell: "Look, friend; none of us are who we appear to be, take me, for example. I used the money that was donated to the so called, Moral Majority to invest in African blood diamonds and Arabian race horses. It wasn't that I didn't ever do good things, hell, I gave people hope and that is something which can <u>not</u> be overvalued."

Elvis: "You got that right, Jerry, you ol' son of a bitch. Now, look here boy. I showed millions of uptight white people how to be cool. I was larger than life. Nobody's bigger than Elvis, even those English boys, or that funny Negro who married my daughter.., son of a bitch. Just look at the charts. But, what the charts won't tell you is that I was an emotionally stunted momma's boy, who couldn't even wipe his own butt. Hell, I died trying just to do that very thing."

Reagan: "My fellow American, in this great nation of ours, a great leader must sometimes do things which make people feel good about themselves. Like when I told Gorbachev, to tear down the Berlin wall. I knew he was already trying to do it, and I saw the CIA report that showed the Soviet Union beginning to implode, six years before I took office. But, the American people needed to believe that the man behind the steering wheel is in control and knows how to make everything right, even if he is acting, a little.

Well, it makes them feel proud, when they see a man who is symbolically great and if you don't give it to them, there will be unrest. As I have said before, my unique contribution to the presidency was to look good from every angle. ...Well, there's that, and the false dilemma that you're either an individualist or a socialist; you either love capitalism or you are the enemy of capitalism. Never- minding that the top ten economies are all a mix of public and private institutions."

John Wayne: "Kid, every cowboy knows when it's time to move the heard. When you see dark clouds on

the horizon you have no choice.
There's right and there's wrong. You
gotta do one or the other. You do the
one and you're living. You do the
other and you're dead as a beaver hat.
Now, that's just a line from one of my
movies, so, don't ask me what the hell
it means. Sometimes being vague, is
all you need.

I inspired generations with my tough
guy bravado. Never mind that the
studio got me deferments from serving
my country in real life and sometimes I
had to fight a few real soldiers to
protect my reputation. I got to be the
hero on the silver screen, partner, and
that is where it really counts."
Jerry: "Just remember
Propagandaman, God blesses those
who bless themselves." (Falwell
winks).

Then a penguin walks out from
between his legs and lays an egg on
Sam's foot. The egg begins to crack
and a serpent with wings, wiggles out
and leaps into the air, growing to

enormous proportions as it flies upward, screeching like a pterodactyl, and blocking out the light of the moon. Then the sky and everything under it went black as a coal mine. The four iconic men circle around him at the four points of the compass and four different colors of light shoot out from their chests, like lightning, red, white, blue, and yellow; sending Sam into a spasming state of trans-fixation.

Sam wakes up suddenly from his sleep and sits up on the edge of the sofa. The penguins on the television are getting ready to jump into the icy water and look for something to eat while avoiding being eaten in return.

Sam turns off the set and wanders into the kitchen, his mind still preoccupied with the dream. In an automatic and neurotic fashion, he opens and closes every cabinet, until settling upon the cool air of the freezer. He then puts his head in completely to enjoy the arctic atmosphere.

After a minute or so, he emerges

with a chicken pot pie, saying the words out load in a high, silly voice, "Chicken pot pie... chickeeen pahht pie." He tosses it into the microwave and turns to stare out the window. The memory of the dream returns to him. "Propagandaman," He says. "Propagandaman??," questioning. Then he strikes a pose with his hands on his hips, chest puffed out and states emphatically, with much drama, "PROPAGANDAMAAAAAN!" He strikes a few more, flexing poses, until he notices that he is being watched by someone mowing their lawn.

Then the microwave beeps and he snaps out of it, responding to the chimes, slowly, as if it were another part of his brain assuming the responsibility for feeding the organism. Moments later, Sam finds himself on the sofa again, an empty pie tin on the table and playing with the remote control.

After flipping through nineteen channels, he stops on a news program, breaking a story about the mysterious person who stopped a streaker at the university. Sam is just catching the end of the segment, so he switches to another channel but he can't find the segment again. Sam is riveted by the possibilities. It is too bizarre to believe and impossible to deny. He remembers being there at exactly, that time. He is certain that it must be himself, but also, very much, not himself. An indescribable fear sets in and Sam shuts of the screen.

He gets up and begins wandering throughout the house, talking to himself out loud. "It's alright... You can get through this... There are professionals who can help you get through this... But this is different... This is…, this is..; I am guinea pig, the accidental guinea pig... I have no idea what has happened and no one is more qualified than I to explain it... (longer pause) There's got to be a.., a workable balance." Sam's uncertainty about the possibilities, seem to be inflating like a

hideously decorated balloon.
"Remember Nash.., when that which is unreal refuses to go away you must ignore it; no engaging. The apparitions of fear can be controlled.., or at least managed... A walk would be good... Yes, yes, a walk... Off we go now, Sam.., into the fresh air."

Sam walks stiffly towards the door and steps out onto the porch. The summer night sky gives him a sense of transitional relief; like he is leaving the presence of a phantom. The air feels good. The further he walks, the more he feels released.

After a few hours of walking, Sam is confronted by a fountain, a minimalist sculpture that also happens to be a fountain. The water flows over the surfaces of limestone, quietly and gently. Sam sits down to listen and to watch. Soon his eyes close; and there is only listening.

After some indeterminate period of time, Sam is struck with the impulse to return to the laboratory. He jumps up and begins moving again.

On the sidewalk he sees a newspaper machine with the headline, "Man Hypnotizes Streaker." There is a photo and he recognizes his profile. He reaches into his pocket but can't find the required change. He tilts the machine toward the light to read the caption. "University streaker brought to a halt by man with unusual voice, suggesting clothing is the norm. (Story on pg. 3). Sam shakes the machine, hoping for a faulty lock, but it doesn't budge. Thinking, there has to be some clue in the software, as to what happened the other day, "It is the primary suspect. The smoking gun sequences have to be there, even If I haven't found them yet."

Arriving at the front gate, he sees the guard through the window. It's the guy from the cafeteria. The guard gets up with curious expression, "Heeey, Mr. R and D, we meet again. How'd you like that book I left you?"

Sam: "I don't think it ever got to me."

He begins to wonder if maybe this was another one of those blackout adventures.

Guard: "Oh, well, I saw what floor you went to the other day and I figured I could always get another copy at the library, so I took the elevator down there and left it on the table."

Sam: "Which table?" (Anxiously).

Guard: "I dunno..; the one in the middle of the room, next to the big machine."

Sam: (With a sharp look of fear, snapping back to fake composure) I'll have to have a look around when I get down there.., Uh... If I see it.., I'll let you know.

Guard: "Alright, I'm here 'til seven. I'm just reading another one I got from Whamazon. It's by Fran Molder, called, "Wasted!" It's about how liberals just want everyone to get stoned and have a good time and don't want anyone to take responsibility for their lives, just live off the government and have sex with anyone, while

preaching the gospel of socialism."
Sam: "Oh.., that sounds very..,
compelling… I'll have to have a look
at it.., someday. Please, excuse me."
Guard: "You bet, Mr. R and D.

Sam walks wide eyed and worried,
towards the inner door. He places his
hand on the finger print scanner and the
door opens.

Down in his lab, he begins looking
through several screen pages to see if
he might be able to better understand
his situation. There are so many lines of
code to look at, it is overwhelming. He
mumbles to himself incoherently.
Eleven hours pass and he feels like
crap. Even with his intimate
understanding of the program, he is
unable to make sense of it. He realizes
that he has to face the harsh reality that
it was the book the guard placed on the
conveyor that made all of this happen.
The combination of exhaustion and
frustration is starting to boil over.
Sam: "That little f*ing twerp and his
sanctimonious, corn-dog, patriotism.

What a piece of sh*t wanna-be, rent-o-cop!!... Oh, I am going to make something very special for you my friend!!

Sam decides to put another book on the conveyor and see what happens. In the back of the lab he has a few shelves of books. Most of them are his, but there are more than a few volumes that were left behind by other people who have used that space. Looking them over, he finds mostly science related stuff but on the bottom shelf there is an old tattered copy of Jack Kerouac's, "On the Road."

Sam: "Oh, this is good…; compete with youthful, acolytic scribblings."

Sam puts the book on the conveyor and smacks the button with the heal of his palm. As the big machine begins to whirr into action, Sam closes his eyes and lets his head fall forward. His face tenses as if to force the outcome. The machine makes weird noises, like free-form jazz in a blender. Five or so minutes pass and it is silent again.

Then there is the tiny sound of a tiny alchemic stone rolling onto the receiving tray. It is metallic like brass, in a hexagonal shape.

Sam looks at the clock. It is 06:38 am. He then picks up the phone and contacts the guard-shack.

Guard: "Hello, security."

Sam: "Hi, this Sam.., I mean.., the guy who works in R and D. We spoke last night when you were first coming on. Do you remember?"

Guard: "Sure, Of course. Did you find the book?"

Sam: "Yes.., yes, I did thank you. It's rather interesting… Hey, I was wondering... I've been working on a new project and it's going to probably going to be the next best thing since Viagra. It hasn't gone through the red tape of big government bureaucracy yet, but you know how that goes."

Guard: "Yeah, they're always trying to interfere and crush the invisible hand of the free market."

Sam: "Yeah.., you got that right...

Anyway, I've been using this product for some time now and so have many of my colleagues here in R and D. And let me tell you this will not only make you last longer, but it will also make you a better lover. So, I was thinking that since I'll be heading home now, I could drop off a sample for you as a token of my gratitude for that amazing book you gave me."

Guard: "I would be honored, sir."

Sam: "Great…, I'll see you soon… Good bye, now."

Guard: "Good bye, sir."

Sam puts the pill in a plastic bag and heads toward the gate. He tries to bring his temper down a bit, so he doesn't give himself away.

Sam: "Hey, how's your shift going?"

Guard: "Not bad, Sir. The nights are my favorite; few interruptions and lots of quiet."

Sam: "I know what you mean. Solitude can be a real blessing sometimes… By the way, my name is Sam."

Guard: "Mine's Cal, short for Calvin."

Sam: "Nice to know you, Cal. Here's the magic bean, I was telling you about. Just make sure you take it on an empty stomach; alright?"

Cal: "Alright, sir.., I mean Sam. And thank you. I'm sure I'm gonna have an interesting weekend."

Sam: "I am sure you will too; bon appetite."

Cal: "Huh?"

Sam: "That just means: enjoy."

Cal: "Thanks."

Sam walks away with a feeling of cheap victory and wonders if his taste for revenge was a waste of his mental resources. Only time will tell.

Chapter Three

A day or so later, it's Monday morning and Sam gets a call from Dr. Soren, the psychotherapist.

Dr. Soren: "Hello this is Dr. Soren. I got your message. I might have called sooner, but I was away for a few days with my family. As often happens on Mondays, I had to reschedule one of my appointments. It's for this afternoon, so if you are still interested, the time is available." Her voice pleasantly modulates.

Sam: Yes, absolutely, thank you for returning my call. Uh.., what time… this afternoon?"

Dr. Soren: "Two o'clock."

Sam: "I can be there… I'll be there. That's great.., but I'm afraid I don't have the address."

Dr. Soren: "It's Thirty-Thirty, Finch Street. Across from the Starlucks and diagonally across from an Italian restaurant called, "Badda Bing Badda Boom."

Sam: "Charming."
Dr. Soren: "Yes, very; but the food is really good, if you're looking for fast and greasy, I can't recommend it enough. There's always a line, though; and it's counter service only."
Sam: "Thanks for the tip. I love Italian, anything."
Dr. Soren: "You're welcome, and I look forward to meeting you."
Sam: "Same here. Thanks again."
Dr. Soren: "Good bye."
Sam: "Good bye."

Sam avoids watching any television for fear of seeing himself again and doesn't leave the house until twenty minutes before the appointment. He arrives with three minutes to spare. The building looks like it might have been a bank in a previous life. Reading the board on the wall inside, he finds her office and heads upstairs. She has a macramé art thing hanging on the door that looks like a childhood art project. The door is partially open and Sam enters to see Dr. Soren in a small side room putting a folder away.

Sam: "Hi, I'm Sam, the two o'clock guy."

Dr. Soren: "Perfect timing. It's nice to meet you." She walks over and invites him to sit."

Sam: "Did Dr. Bradlebaum mention anything to you about what has been happening with me?"

Dr. Soren: "No, not yet. It's been a while since I've heard from him actually."

Sam: "O.k., well let me just get right to the point then... I do research in chemistry and electronics and about five days ago, I accidentally consumed something which has altered my behavior but, I have been completely unaware of those experiences, as they are taking place."

Dr. Soren: "How have you come to find out about those changes then?"

Sam: "Have you seen the news lately?"

Dr. Soren: "No, I didn't take in any news while I was away."

Sam: "Then, you are probably going to think I am insane and want to have me institutionalized."

Dr. Soren: "Are you concerned about your own safety or the safety of others?"

Sam: "No, as it turns out, the things I do when I am in that altered state, are relatively benign, depending on your political leanings."

Dr. Soren: "I don't understand."

Sam: "Neither do I, but it appears that I have acquired a… special ability to influence people."

Dr. Soren: "What kind of influence?"

Sam: "Well, the first time it happened, that I know of, I apparently convinced an entire park full of protesters to pack it up and go home… and the police, who were about to raid them with tear gas, loved it."

Dr. Soren: "And you saw this on the news, you say?"

Sam: "Yes and so did Dr. Bradlebaum, He said I was using a propaganda technique known as, "The big lie," which is the repetition of something so outrageous and untrue, that people are shocked into believing it."

Dr. Soren: "Did he know what it is, that you said."

Sam: "I'm not sure, not precisely, anyhow. I saw the news coverage and it was difficult to make out… and the police officer on the scene, seemed confused… And well, yesterday afternoon, it happened again and this time I saw a newspaper article which proclaimed that I had thwarted a streaker with the suggestion that clothing is the norm and not nudity."

Dr. Soren: "That's known as 'bandwagoning'."

Sam: "And what does that mean?"

Dr. Soren: "Basically, it's language… that is used to promote conformity to mass movements and…, while playing on feelings of isolation or missing out."

Sam: "And that's propaganda too, I take it."

Dr. Soren: "Yes, one of the more common ones."

Sam: "Do you really believe anything that I am telling you right now? If I wasn't so desperate, I might be inclined to think that you were patronizing me in some way... Though, if I were in your shoes I would probably patronize me, too."

Dr. Soren: "Whether or not I believe you, is inconsequential at this point. Sometimes a person needs to use illusion... to escape illusion. Either way, it requires a similar approach... What I mean is, it can be useful to explore all the terrains of thought to discover the most viable paths."

Sam: "So, maybe I should get a cape and a pair of tights, so I can use my special powers to fight crime."

Dr. Soren: "Have you ever been to a therapist before?"

Sam: "No."

Dr. Soren: "Well, I am not going to gaslight you. That is to say…, I will not lead you to believe that you are crazy and need my help, just so I can keep your business. So, if you are going to trust me, it must be on terms which you find agreeable. We won't make progress if I aggressively challenge your perceptions."

Sam: "You're right.., sorry about the sarcasm."

Dr. Soren: "Why don't you tell me what it was that you took?"

Sam: "Well, this is where it gets weird.., I mean, weirder... I'm not supposed to be telling you any of this because of my contract, but it isn't an issue of national security."

Dr. Soren: "For what it's worth, I don't discuss my work with others. It would also put my career in jeopardy."

Sam: "How, ironic."

Soren: "Yes, but it's not about money, necessarily; it's about people...and helping them... to cope."

Sam: "I'll try not to let my cynicism get in the way."

Dr. Soren: "Fair enough."

Sam: "O.k.., on the very day when I was finishing the project I have been working on for almost seven years..., which would revolutionize the way drug companies extend their patents, by automatically making copy-cat drugs… Well, some political zealot, security guard, left one of his stupid books near the machine I built, and this is going to sound very bizarre but.., it went into the processor and the machine produced something… it was never intended to produce… And I didn't see him do it so I made the false assumption that it was performing according to design and now, here I am."

Dr. Soren: "Please, continue."

Sam: "Well, the machine turned the book into a pill; I don't know how…, but that is the only conclusion I can come to… And because I didn't see it happen, I thought it was merely a variation of the previous run, which I was eager to test on myself, but due to my careless overconfidence, I took the wrong one."

Dr. Soren: "What did you think it was?"

Sam: "Just some aphrodisiac, like

Vergara or Ciara."

Dr. Soren: "But you assimilated the information from the book?"

Sam: "I wish that were the case, then, I could challenge the information, internally, just as I challenge all thinking that doesn't quite match objective reality. It seems that it has taken over a part of my brain and manifests as an alternative persona, like a Mr. Hyde."

Dr. Soren: "Have you thought of putting another book through your machine to counteract it or balance it out?"

Sam: "Yes.., but it might make things worse and I don't know if I am prepared to endure a combination which might enhance Mr. Hyde."

Dr. Soren: "Probably any book on logic could be useful, or maybe Jaques Ellul's book, titled, 'Propaganda, the formation of men's attitudes'. It is a classic. I don't have a copy, but it would be easy to find. Of course, the decision to use it will be one you have to make for yourself."

Sam: "I am beginning to think that I don't have any other options."

Dr. Soren pauses, not wanting to interrupt Sam's contemplation.

Sam: "O.k., I'm gonna do it; I have to. And I would like to make another appointment for two weeks from now, if possible."

Dr. Soren: "Sure, we can at least do another short session like this one, at the very least. If you require more time though, that might take some shuffling."

Sam: "Of course, and thank you seeing me on such short notice. I really appreciate it."

Dr. Soren: "You're welcome… and good luck."

Sam: "Yeah, that's pretty much what it comes down to."

Dr. Soren: "Good bye Sam. Take care."

Sam: "Good bye."

Chapter Four

Sam moves through the street with assurance in his stride. The sun is out and the glow builds up his sense of purpose. Four blocks later he is at the library trolling the shelves for prospects. He finds they have two copies of the Jaques Ellul book on propaganda and he also finds books titled, "Obedience to authority, by Stanley Milgram, "The psychology of judgment and decision making" by Scott Plous, and an omnibus of Aristotle's founding texts on Logic, "The Organon." Sam quickly checks out the books thinking he would rather get this done now and pay for the books in fines, than wait any longer.

Sam arrives at the lab gate after a short drive that was elongated by traffic, and is confronted by another guard; yet another unfamiliar face. The guard gets up and approaches him with a large envelope. "Are you Sam Hyam? **Sam:** "I am."

Guard: "I was told to give you this and to tell you that you are not allowed to enter the building... Oh, and I need you to turn in your security pass."

Sam: "I don't understand. Are you sure you have the right guy?"

Guard: "They put a picture of you with your pass number on the wall of the guard shack. That's how I know... And if your pass number matches the one on this envelope ...I am sorry to have to be the one to do this to you. I have a box with your stuff inside"

Sam: "I'm just feeling completely blindsided by all of this. I can't even begin to imagine what is going on."

Sam hands his security pass to the guard. The guard compares it and hands him the envelope then goes to get the box. Sam's face is blank.

Guard: "Look I'm really sorry. You seem like a decent enough guy. I'm just doin my job."

Sam: "Yeah., it's just…. never mind."

Sam turns and walks away. A block later he stops and sits to open the envelope. It contains a few pages and a check in the amount of 2.7 million dollars. The cover letter explains that under the conditions of his contract all samples and or results were to be submitted for review to the research board and in the event of his non-compliance, the board was free to make a determination about the future of his involvement in the project. There was no explanation about what event they were implying, but it didn't matter now.

Sam gets up and walks until he finds a bar and proceeds to tie one on. The place is simple and well worn. It's Just before the dawn of happy hour and he is the only customer. The bartender is a short, sixty something guy with thick white curly hair and tired eyes.

Sam: "I've never been much of a drinker, but I've heard, from college lore, that the Long Island Ice Tea is very effective."

Bartender: "Sure as a Xantippe on a Xargumentondo, mister."

Sam: "Huh?" This nonsensical comment almost makes Sam smile. "O.k., I'll take two."

Bartender: "You got it."

Twenty minutes pass before another customer enters the bar and Sam is well on his way to his Xargumentondo. He is almost halfway through the second drink and a man sits down a few seats over and closer to the television. He gives Sam a funny look but Sam doesn't notice.

Bartender: "Hi-ya, Tommy, how's business?"

Tommy: "I've seen better days, Mike, but our ball club is startin to get their mojo workin, so I'm a happy camper."

Mike: "Yeah, it looks like Johnson is on the path to becoming a hall of famer."

He pours Tommy a beer without mentioning it and sets it on the counter. Tommy shoots Sam another quick look. Again, Sam doesn't notice.

Tommy: "I know who you are." He says to Sam.

Sam: (Swiveling his head loosely)
"That makes one of us."

Tommy: (Addressing both men) "He's
that guy who's been in the news lately,
the one who broke up that protest at the
park and stopped the streaker at the
university."

Sam: "I'm not so sure that was me."

Tommy: "Whatta you mean, it's gotta
be you. You look just like him.
Doesn't he look like that guy, Mike?"

Mike: "Maybe, but maybe he just
wants to be left alone, ya know?"

Sam: "It's alright. I've got nothing to
hide now, anyhow. It's alright. My
contract just got dissolved and my life's
work just got snatched away from me
by a bunch of corporate whores. Yeah,
I'm the guy.., I'm that guy.., f*ck it.
But don't ask me what it means. It's
just some kinda Twilight Zone sh*t.. I
don't know"

Tommy: "Well my brothers on the
force and he says they all think they
witnessed a miracle."

Sam: "Praise Jesus, I got a bunch of

people to surrender their freedom to assemble and freedom of speech, but who gives a crap. They're all a bunch of useless eaters anyhow, right? Maybe we should just spray paint a big X right in the middle of the flag."

Tommy: "You saved them from gettin their heads bashed in and you saved the tax payers a lot of money for overtime police duties."

Sam: "Oh, well., that's important too. I wouldn't want to be accused of not being fair and balanced. I guess you're right., I might as well face it, I am a miracle worker for the government. Yes., I shouldn't resist it any longer, I will go out right now and hold a press conference, so that everyone will be forewarned not to challenge the system."

Tommy: "Hey, could I get your autograph. My brother is gonna flip when I tell him that I met you."

Sam: "Sure, no problem."

Tommy passes him a dry paper coaster and Sam signs it,

"Propagandaman," with bold lines and underscores.

Tommy: "Propagandaman, what kind of name is that?"

Sam: "It's Greek."

He then gets up and heads for the door with his box.

After several blocks of wandering with a dazed expression, Sam comes across a comic book store and is struck with a sense of synchronicity. He stands for a moment, still rather intoxicated, and revels at the images and displays in the windows; colorful, mythological Gods and Goddesses exploding into action. He wonders if his new, stranger half is being evoked by this or if it's just the booze. What does it matter? He thinks, if you must lose your mind you might as well have some fun with it, and he enters.

The guy behind the counter is busy arguing with someone over some minutiae about which superhero has the least interesting abilities.

Clerk: "Batman doesn't have any

special abilities, so he doesn't count. You have to have special abilities first, before determining whether or not they are interesting."

Customer: "But he's rich."

Clerk: "So is George W. Bush. He might be special, but where are the abilities."

Customer: "Touché… What about Iceman, all he does is freeze stuff. It's only interesting if someone runs out of ice at a party."

Clerk: "You're right, that is pretty lame. Hang on, someone else is here." He addresses Sam, "Can I help you find anything?"

Sam: "I don't know where to begin."

Clerk: "Well, you're welcome to look around, but I have to ask you to leave the box up here., store policy."

Sam: "Oh, sure." He sets it on the counter and wanders around. He looks at the covers on display, second guessing why the hell he is in such a place.

After bumbling around for a while,

looking with amusement at several splashy covers, he comes across an old copy of "The Shadow" detective magazine from July 15th, 1939 in a glass case. Sam is taken by the image of a man wearing a wide brimmed hat with a suit and a cape. The magazine has a folded card next to it, indicating the price is $200.00. "Excuse me", Sam calls to the Clerk, "Do you know anything about this one?"

Clerk: "What would you like to know?"

Sam: "Well.., what's it about?. What does the character do?"

Clerk: "I haven't read it, but I know that the Shadow has special powers of hypnosis and can even cloud men's minds to the point where he effectively becomes invisible… Oh, and he can also mimic people.., their voices, that is, as well as being a master of disguise and slight-of hand."

Sam: "I like it. I'll take this one."

Clerk: "Of course, I'll get the key."

Sam: "Thank you."

While the clerk is ringing it up, Sam notices a costume on the wall behind the counter. It is blue body suit with a red cape and red boots. In the center of the chest is a capital letter, "B". Sam asks, "What's the story behind the suit?", pointing.

Clerk: "It belongs to a friend of mine. It was for a character from a book that he was trying to promote. It's about a Franciscan monk who leaves the monastery to fight crime in the inner city by being really friendly and nice to everyone, setting an example."

Sam: "How idealistic."

Clerk: "He would have agreed with you. His opinion was that ideals are the goals towards which we must move, even if and especially if it seems hopeless."

Sam: "Sort of a romantic struggle against nihilism and meaninglessness."

Clerk: "Exactly."

Sam: "What does the "B" stand for?"

Clerk: "Brother-man."

Sam: "Really, (chuckling) that's pretty

funny."

Clerk: "That's what I thought. It could have had a following if he saw the humor in it and went with that in mind."

Sam: "How much do you want for it?"

Clerk: "Like I said it doesn't really belong to me, we just put it up for decoration."

Sam: "I'll give you five hundred."

Clerk: "Done."

Outside, Sam hails a taxi and heads home.

Later that evening, he is at home, eating Chinese delivery-shrimp egg foo young, drinking whiskey, and reading comfortably in his living room. After finishing the magazine, he is feeling heady about the prospect of coming to terms with the powers which have been fated to him. He is figuring, once again, that he might be in the process of surrendering to something he cannot possibly fight.

Then standing before the mirror in his new outfit, with the letter "B" now converted to a "P", the reality of what he is contemplating seems like a joke. He laughs and then says aloud, "Is this not revenge? This is not even close to justice." Then something in him seems to gradually turn and twist in his mind. "Oh, but they will see what I am capable of. When they see what I have done, the memory of me will ripple across their brains like a tsunami. I will show them power, like they have never witnessed it before. I will have global corporations eating from the palm of my hand and politicians groveling at my feet." Then he begins to laugh some more and the sinister amusement of it leaves him cackling like a crazy man.

Chapter Five

Sam heads out on the street as Propagandaman, in full uniform. Any feeling of awkwardness is overpowered by half-crazed determination. People he passes look with amusement but this only feeds his sense of destiny. And his first destination is Leslie's apartment. He strides up the stairs and rings the bell with authority. A moment later she is calling through the door to ask who it is and he responds with a manly tone, "It is I, Propagandaman."

Leslie: "Sam..?" Recognizing his voice, she opens the door.

As soon she sees him, she breaks out into laughter; the kind of laughter that is so out of control that it usually causes a disruption.

Sam: "Leslie, it's not that funny... Are you high?"

Leslie: (Struggling to speak) "I am now; (More laughter) Oh, my god, where did you get that outfit?"

Sam: "I found it at a comic book store near Lake Street… I lost my job today.

Leslie: "Really?" (Suddenly calming)

Sam: "Yeah, when I showed up at the gate this afternoon, the guard made me turn-in my pass and gave me an envelope with some vague explanation and a check, along with a box filled with my stuff."

Leslie: "That's terrible, after all you put into that project. What makes them think they can just push people around like that? What a bunch of A-holes!"

Sam: "They have a legion of lawyers and I don't. Even if I had a case, which I'm pretty sure I don't, they would make things so hard for me, that I'd wish I had gone into truck driving instead of research."

Leslie: "So, is this your way of protesting or celebrating?"

Sam: "Both.., I'm reinventing myself."

Leslie: "So, you're going to entertain at children's birthday parties?

(chuckling) Have you been drinking?"

Sam: "Yes, but it's wearing off. Do you remember the video on the morning news?"

Leslie: "Yes, of course."

Sam: "Well, it turns out, that <u>was</u> me. The pill I took the last time we were together has done something to me which makes it possible for me to influence people with word tricks or something like that."

Leslie: "So, that's what the "P" is for. I thought I heard you correctly the first time, ropagandaman. Don't you think that is a little over the top? I mean, is the costume really necessary?"

Sam: "I want to capture the imagination of the people. I'm going to get even with Phiz-bang in the only way that I can."

Leslie: "So you're going to turn popular sentiment against them?"

Sam: "I don't know yet, probably something like that... Look, I'm not going to be around for a while. I'm confused and maybe even losing my

mind. I just didn't want to leave
without saying good bye."

Leslie: (Concerned) "Are you breaking
up with me?"

Sam: "I don't know... All I know is
things are about to get really strange
and I don't want to get you tangled up
in it."

Leslie: "Why don't you take a break
and think about it for a few days?
Maybe we can spend some time
together, take a vacation for a change
and then... you can deal with this in a
more rational way."

Sam: "I appreciate your appeal to
reason, but I just can't be rational any
more. Good-bye Leslie." He turns to
leave.

Leslie: "Wait." Sam looks. "Have
you noticed that some people are not
affected by what you say..., I mean like
in the video?"

Sam: "Your right but, how the hell
should I know? Maybe I'm directing it
somehow. Maybe it doesn't work on
borderline socio-paths... I can't think

about this right now."

Leslie stares as drifts on.

Sam wants to put his powers to the test some more and see what happens. Eventually he makes his way to the more dangerous side of town. It doesn't take long for him to run into a group of young people hanging out on a street corner and the baiting begins.

Thug 01: "Yo, check it out. Superman is lost."

Thug 02: "That's not Superman. He got a "P" on his chest. He mus be Pooper-man." (Laughter).

Thug 03: "No, yo, this dude be Pimp-man, Only a pimp would dress like that. Hey Pimp-man, you tryin to move in on our territory? You betta got you some supa powers or you gonna get messed up, yo." (more laughter)

Sam is ready for the challenge like never before and starts to throw down.

Propagandaman: "You got that right, yo. (Rhythmically rapping)
I'z the pimpinest pimp from the ghetto to the strip.

You got a problem with that, then yo headz bout to trip."
(One of the thugs starts beat boxing and P-man busts a move).
"You betta call out yo Bloods and call out yo Crips.
Because it's history I'm flow-in and it's 'bout to get sick.
When the helicopters come wit they cameras and lights,
I'm gonna boggle they mindz with a mystical sight.
With they Glocks still cold and no itch fo a fight,
I'll have them whiggin like shorties on Christmas Eve night.
Ain't no Santa Claus ever had a game so tight.
Because I'm Propagandaman and I makes everythang right.
Now, who dat?"
Crowd: "Yooo!, Propagandaman!"
P-man: "Who dat?"
Crowd: "Yooo!, Propagandaman!"
P-man: "I say now, who dat?"
Crowd: "Yooo!, Propagandaman!"

P-man: "Tell everybody in the hee-zee Propagandaman is here.

But there's just one thing that I gots to make clear.

Now, if you got some anger and if you gots fear,

I'll use it all against you, right into next year.

You can't run. You can't hide. I got psy-ops on my side.

Twistin heads like a pretzel, til yo thoughts all collide.

You will never know what hit you, not even know why.

But your will is now my toy and this cannot be denied.

Now, who dat?"

Crowd: "Yooo!, Propagandaman!"

P-man: "Who dat?"

Crowd: "Yooo!, Propagandaman!"

P-man: "I say now, who dat?"

Crowd: "Yooo!, Propagandaman!"

P-man: …"You got that right."

Crowd: "Hhhmmmmm!" (All with arms folded, ala, Run DMC).

And with that the Propagandaman is gone; once again leaving people wondering, if what happened was real.

As he is walking across town, he realizes that there was something different that time. Not only was he able to tailor the message perfectly for the audience, but he was aware of it the whole time. He didn't black out. Something must have happened in his neurological networks to adjust to the chemicals. Or maybe the dream had something to do with it. What more was to come, he wonders, anticipating.

The moon is full and low in the sky; almost like in the dream. He walks to the center of a bridge to get a better view of the reflection off the water. Time seems to slow down, more and more, as he listens to the soft flowing sound of the waves. In the open air, the reverberation of the city backdrop drifts away, along with its urgencies. He begins thinking about a song from the 80's, "I can feel it coming in the air tonight, oh Lord... And I've been waiting for this moment for all my life…" A smile emerges from inside of him and he begins to snicker; then this turn into all out laughter. He begins shaking his head and thinks, now I have a soundtrack in my head. It doesn't get any more surreal than this.

He goes into a convenience store to get some Armadillo-aide, a sports drink with electrolytes, to ease off the effect of his hang-over. He is a bit tired, but his adrenaline will not quit. Before he closes the refrigerator door a man enters with a mask and a pistol and commences to hold the place up. Propagandaman sees him in the mirror and nonchalantly walks towards the counter, sipping his drink.

Robber: "Who the F*#@ are you?!!" (With a distinctive Appalachian accent.)

P-man: (Matching the accent) "I'm just a man of humble upbringin. My daddy worked like a dog all his life and could barely put food on the table. While my momma did everything she could to make sure I would grow up to have a better life. Unfortunately, she got tuberculosis when I was still a young-un and it took her life. My daddy and me went from place to place, getting by as best we knew how, coal minin, brick layin, ditch digin, farm pickin, it didn't matter what. And he used to say to me, "Son, there ain't no shame in an honest days work. No matter how hard it gets, it's never as hard as the life of crime." I never got me any o' that book learnin my momma wanted me to have. No, I'm just plain folks. But I know what it's like to struggle with dignity, with my head held high." At this point the robber lowers his pistol and begins to weep.

Robber: "That's just like my story. You remine me of my brother, except he didn't have a cape or no fancy tight suit. He was real good, ya know? We grew up in West Virginia and it was good even when it was bad. I didn't know how good I had it. I don't know where I went wrong. "

P-man: "Well, I know where you can go right ...Just put down that gun and lift your hands where those fine police officers comin in behind you, can see em, and maybe this local proprietor will be kind-nuff to let bygones be bygones." The robber then puts down his gun and surrenders to the police. While the police are hand cuffing him, one of them says, "Hey aren't you that guy from Talinni park?"

P-man: "Yes, that was me."

Cop: "So, you're some kind of superhero. I knew it all along. What do call yourself?"

P-man: "Propagandaman... and things are about to get very interesting around this here town."

Chapter Six

What would have been a normal, and boring news day cycle is now become a feeding frenzy. The convenience store, camera images are being played repeatedly, along with the testimonial of the store clerk.

Clerk: (With a South Pacific accent). "I did not know what it was happening. He was only talking, talking to the robber, telling him story and then the robber just give himself up."

Reporter: "Do you remember anything that he said?"

Clerk: "He said, 'I am a plain folks'… and his father worked very, very hard to support him… and his mother died when he was young. And his father said to him, 'Son, hard work is much easier than hard crime.' That is all I can remember, it was so special… Oh, then he said to the policeman, 'I am Propagandaman.' Then he went out of the store."

Sam is watching all of this from a distance, amused and satisfied with the way people are reacting. Scheming about what his next move will be and how this event could lead him to it. Later in the day, someone from the street gang comes forward to get a little of that celebrity for a day, free air-time for himself.

Gangbanger: "It was like crazy man. It was like, we was dissin him an all that, an he jus dropped it, propper dopper man. P-man was straight up dope, yo. He was rappin some sh(beep) like psy-ops and choppers, and Santa Claus with the street gangs. It was some trippy sh(beep), yo. My peeps is all diffren now. I don know how to splain it. But somephin happened. They like, lookin fo sometin else to do wit thay lives now, yo. But it's cool. We cool. We kickin it, old school."

Reporter: "There you have it. (Stiffly) 'P-man was straight up dope, yo.'; back to you, Angela."

Angela: "He is the man that the whole country seems to be talking about; The mysterious real life super hero, known as Propagandaman. The Eyewitness news team will keep you updated as events unfold. But up next, the kitten who thinks she is a pit-bull and won't take no, for an answer." (Clip of kitten playing rough with a pit-bull).

Sam then waits for several days for the hysteria to ferment a little. He is staying home and watching with great reverie as the commentators and pundits waste their breath in speculation. The events are being spoofed on comedy shows as well as on the internet; a mocking rap video is starting to go viral. Sam orders take-out from every restaurant in the neighborhood, observing and plotting the possibilities.

On Tuesday morning, Sam puts on some sunglasses and a baseball cap and heads to the post office to rent a box with the phony business name, 'Excalibur Communication Services'.

In the afternoon, he goes to a ticket-broker's office and purchases a front row reservation, with cash, to see 'Satan's Gay Babies,' in concert, a moderately successful heavy rock band from the Pacific Northwest.

When the day of the show arrives, Sam is early and waiting in his seat, just as the sound check is ending. He is wearing a long beige coat and reading a book called 'The Power of Persuasion'.

Gradually the fans file in, flaunting the style of outsider's outsiders: more body piercings per person, than can fit in a fishing tackle box and enough tattoos to wallpaper a small bathroom. There is a certain giddiness in the air that can only be described as the solidarity of the strange.

Just before the band comes out, Sam throws off his coat and leaps on to the stage in his costume. At first, the theatrics of this seem planned and the response is one of amusement. They aren't sure if this is the guy who's been all over the media. Then he begins to speak into the microphone with a steady, serious tone: "America is your heritage, (pause) freedom is your tradition, (pause) family is your fortune, (pause) patriotism is your privilege, (pause) God is your gift, (pause) flag is forever, (pause) and exceptionalism is your greatness."

At first the crowd is laughing at the silliness of these glittering and meaningless generalities, but as he continues to repeat the words, a vague state of mystifying stupor begins to set in.

"America is your heritage, (pause) freedom is your tradition, (pause) family is your fortune, (pause) patriotism is your privilege, (pause) god is your gift, (pause) flag is forever, (pause) and exceptionalism is your greatness."

The venue manager is about to radio security, to put an end to this, but he too, is affected by the words in a way that interrupts his concentration.

"America is your heritage, (pause)

freedom is your tradition, (pause) family is your fortune, (pause) patriotism is your privilege, (pause) god is your gift, (pause) flag is forever, (pause) and exceptionalism is your greatness."

Slowly the crowd is beginning to recite the words with him. Sam instructs the crowd to stand up and chant the words louder and louder. He has commandeered an audience of nearly three thousand social misfits with a message that is antithetical to this cultural milieu, and Sam's confidence is soaring.

Shortly he instructs them follow him out of the venue and on to the street. The band members also follow, each chanting: "America is your heritage, (pause) freedom is your tradition, (pause) family is your fortune, (pause) patriotism is your privilege, (pause) god is your gift, (pause) flag is forever, (pause) and exceptionalism is your greatness."

The parade builds quickly and the

attention of cameras soon follows. This is media Nirvana, a mass of humanity (albeit, outsider, humanity) doing something which defies explanation. Oh, this has been done before, but never so instantaneously. Usually, there is a manufactured crisis and there is a certain built in, willingness, lying dormant beneath the fertile facades of John and Jane Doe, to participate in their own manipulation. Tonight the stories are being written, many are improvised, but this night the world changes. This is when the so called, power brokers and gate keepers take notice. The significance of this man's gift is un-ignorable as well as unnatural.

For the next few days the news cycles are awash with the images. What was already out of control has become a worldwide obsession. T-shirts and trinkets are being manufactured. Conspiracy theories are being spun. The so-called, right is accusing the so-called, left and the so-called left is

accusing the so-called, right.
Meanwhile, corporate executives are arguing about how they can cash in on this remarkable young man's talents, but what they don't realize is that there are other motives at work here.

Later, Sam is writing a general letter,
"To whom it may concern:

The person who has been dominating media coverage for the past three days is my client, and his services are available at a rate of one million dollars minimum, with priority going to the highest bidder. This service includes total domination of one's market sector and a solid, non-compete contract. Those who find this unaffordable might want to consider selling their businesses to those who don't, before they are left with no choice.

Seriously,
The Legal Representation for Propagandaman.

P.O. Box, 5057, New York, NY 10002

The letter goes out to 100 of the top businesses in the country. And twelve days later, Sam is looking at just one envelope from a cola company. The letter explains basically, that they are sorry, but at this time they will not be in need of his services. He thought it was odd that they felt compelled to reply at all and that maybe it was time for demonstration.

He heads home and gets a camera out of the closet, then gets a glass of water from the tap, turns on the camera, and begins his psychological transfer, pitch: "This is a glass of water. It is about 65% of who you are, and yet, so few people drink it. Why would anyone spend money for a beverage which nature has already perfected? And it's virtually free! I just got this from my tap and it is delicious (Sam takes a slow drink). Mmmm! My body is my temple and I don't drink anything else."

He posts the video on the internet and within 22 hours the stocks on all beverage companies collapse. The acceleration time in the news cycle to the national and international stage is doubling. Now there is a note on his P.O. Box which reads, "Please come to the desk." There is nothing inside the box again, but when he goes to the desk, they give him three big canvass bags and a deposit bill for the return of the bags.

At home Sam is sorting the piles into four categories: those with a corporate logo, those with a media logo, those with a government logo, and those with no logo. It's funny how interconnected everyone is, he thought. First priority is the money. Find the highest bidder first. Three hours later, he says aloud, "And the winner is, no surprise, from the top of the fortune 500 list, and the largest retailer on the planet, Wally-town! Admittedly, not a beverage company, but the bevies will have to wait." Wally-town offered him

112 million, which is a drop in the bucket for them.

Sam arrives at the meeting in full costume.

Sam: "You asked for a proposal, and here it is. A series of 'reality commercials', which show me interacting with your staff and the camera, with the intention of showing the Wally-town experience as one of adventure and community."

Advertising Executive: "I love it! That's brilliant."

Sam: "I am Propagandaman, This is what I do."

Executive #2: "Have you done any statistical analysis for a comprehensive marketing strategy? I know that you are very popular right now, but how can we be confident that you understand who our target demographics are? Or, are you just going to wing it? (He said with a tone of condescension)."

Sam: "I don't think you fully realize who you are dealing with. If I chose to,

I could convert you into a radical Islamic fundamentalist and within a week you would be contemplating a suicide bombing. But then, what fun would that be? I think it would be much more interesting to watch as you transform into the most devout Jainist the world has ever known and revel at how easy it is for the human mind to surrender without scrutiny to utter self-abasement, renouncing all of your worldly possessions, and agonizing over your desire to live a normal human life, whatever that is.

Even as you are listening to the sound of my voice, you can find that place inside of yourself where tolerance to the viewpoints of others is so strong, that it puts you instantly into a state of innocence, like that of a child. It is becoming easier and easier to seek only agreement with others, and your greatest pleasure is non-confrontation or peace at all costs."

A glazed expression appeared on the man's face as Sam was speaking and he began removing articles of value from his person and placing them on the table: his rings, watch, tie pin, cufflinks, and wallet. Then scooping them up with both hands, he looks around the room with gravity and says, "I must go feed the poor." Then he leaves immediately, never to return.

The rest of the executives are stunned. For a moment, nobody makes a sound. They stare blankly, almost afraid to make eye contact with each other. Then Sam speaks: "We'll start shooting tomorrow. Any further questions?"

Lead Exec: No., no, that will be fine. Allow me to write you a cheque; if that is an acceptable form of payment?"

Sam: "Yes that will be fine."

The following day, we see Propagandaman gliding down the aisles of Wally-town, doing acrobatic tricks with the cart (with the help of wires). Then the camera cuts to a **close up:** "I'm gettin my Wally-town on!" Next, he's conversing with a grocer, "How much is this pumpkin?"

Grocer: "Sir, I believe that is a tomato, and they are three for a dollar."

Sam: "Hey, that's a great deal! You think I don't know the difference between tomatoes and pumpkins. I grew up on a farm, you city slicker!" Next, he is conducting a conga dance line through the middle of the store, with employees and customers having a blast, while the music of Tito Puente plays over the sound system. Next, Propagandaman is standing in front of the store with the cast and crew gathered around him. The camera jib crane starts in close and pulls up and away as he says with great verve, "Wally-town is not just about people, it's about life." And they all throw their arms up with a shout, while a single symphonic chord plays triumphantly.

Never in the history of the human species has such a cultural phenomenon been witnessed. This is like the invention of writing, the industrial revolution, and the age of information, combined, with a dose of steroids and LSD, as they say. With amazing speed, the already Mega-powerful, Wally-town becomes a force which cannot be stopped. No other such business can compete and it is once again on the forefront of all news outlets. As P-man promised, there can be only one.

The following commercial he produces is for the car/truck company, Generic Motors: It features him chopping wood on the tailgate of his pick-up truck, having a barbeque party on the tailgate of his pick-up truck, doing a swan dive into a country pond from the tailgate of his pick-up truck, making a marriage proposal from the tailgate of his pick-up truck, having a wedding ceremony on the tailgate of his pick-up truck, then delivering a baby on the tailgate of his pick-up truck, and finally a funeral with a casket in the back of his pick-up truck, being lowered into the ground. Then, P-man delivers the voice over, "For every chapter of your life, we will be there; because, we are Generic Motors." Then a hand reaches up through the ground of the burial site.

Worthy of note was the ad that he does for The Unconscionably Big Bank of American Awesomeness. It only shows him standing in front of a wall of money, flanked by men in suits. He says simply, "We're not too big to fail. We're too big not to bail." Then he winks and salutes as the image merges with a waving flag. He then adds, "Capitalism is the definition of America."

The oddest one was the spot that he did for the computer programming company, Macrohard; he is sitting near a glowing computer in the dark when the commercial starts. Then he turns toward the camera as the lights slowly come on and says, "Nothing gets my macros hard like Macrohard. Number thirty-five on the fortune 500, beeeyatches!" Then he spins in his chair towards the glow of a computer screen, while swanky music plays and the light, fades. Nevertheless, the stock shoots up.

Eventually, a whining beverage company makes an offer that is worth his time and he decides to save them from utter ruin. He meets with the executives, tells them precisely how the ad campaign is going to be executed and which account to wire the money to. Three days later, the commercial is aired. He is wearing a psychedelic outfit, walking toward the camera, and then he stops and says, "If someone told me there was a beverage which could separate me from my closest friends, I'd say…, 'I'd like to try that'." Then he holds up a red can with white letters that read, "Yoko-Cola", and he begins guzzling, while the liquid drips all over him. Incidentally, he insisted on the name change.

These volatile trends in the so-called free market continue for several months when he is contacted by a courier who has been following him. "The business slash political powerhouse oil baron duo, known as the Cox brothers want to offer you a billion dollars, for a two part campaign to malign the science of green energy and to permanently fix the frame of global warming as a conspiratorial liberal hoax." Sam turns to look at the man with extreme incredulity, "My background is in science. Believe it or not, on most days I value evidence very highly. If ninety-seven doctors told you, that you had cancer, while three said you have nothing to worry about; who would you listen to?" The man says nothing.

Sam: "Exactly. Well, this is the way it breaks down in the scientific community; 97 percent to 3 percent. The Cox brothers' request is not only unethical but it is self-destructive. I cannot cross that line."

Chapter Seven

Several days have passed and Sam is intoxicated and increasingly irresponsible with his new found power. There is a nagging sense of distance from the person he used to be. If dreams of science, as a cause were being manifested, they stayed out of the range of his conscious reflection. Until the phone rings and it is Leslie.

Sam: "Hi Leslie"

Leslie: "I have always been respectful of your need for solitude.

Sam: "Just like your father, right?"

Leslie: (Sweetly) Shut up Freud, I need to tell you this. Your determination and brilliance are things that I admire and you know it; but I feel compelled to tell you as a fellow human being. that you are violating your own standards of decency."

Sam: "I know where you are going with this."

Leslie: "I do not intend this as a statement of judgment. I only wish to remind you of the sort of man that you used to be. If you saw someone behaving publicly, as you have been behaving, you would not withhold your ridicule."

Sam: (after a long pause, with patience from Leslie) "I can't argue with you. But I feel like I have my back against the wall... The work which I have sacrificed so much for has been yanked away from me, and all I have left is this weird ability to create mass hysteria... I can't see a clear path to where I began. It is as if... the path and I..., have been erased. How could I be anything other than cynical?"

Leslie: "It would be absurd for me to begin, even a short campaign to convince you of the virtues of problem solving techniques. That is your area of expertise."

Sam: "It would probably be more accurate to say that problems possess me…, at least until I can exorcise them."

Leslie: "Whatever. The thing that you are missing, the thing you don't appreciate, is that I deal with people all the time; small vulnerable people, who are not sure what to make of the world around them. And part of what I do is, help them to understand and to not be afraid. To ask questions with the confidence, that those who appear to have authority can sometimes be an ally, that the world is not necessarily a threat and that engagement with the cultural environment around you can be fulfilling."

Sam: "I do appreciate that, but right now…, I am dealing with grown-ups."

Leslie: "Are you sure about that?

Sam: "Most of them."

Leslie: "Are the grown-ups, the ones with the most cash and political influence?"

Sam: "O.K., debate team cap-E-tan; you win. I will go to the CEO of Phizbang, tomorrow.

Leslie: "Are you going to persuade him to give you your job back?"

Sam: "I don't need that job or any other job. I am making millions as a consultant."

Leslie: "Is that what you're calling it now…, consulting?"

Sam: "You know what I mean…, but never mind that, I just want to gain access to my project."

Leslie: "Oh, O.K.… Well, I have to go check on something in the kitchen."

Sam: "Are you cooking something, or are you just brushing me off?"

Leslie: "Yeah…, I'm baking some bread. And it smells like it's almost done…, but honestly, we are on two different paths now, ethically speaking, so, let's just say that, if you had any religious world-view, I would have to say that I have no have hope for your soul. And why would such a worldly man be interested in someone like me?"

Sam: "You're not using a timer?"

Leslie: "For the bread, no, I improvised with some of the ingredients and I don't want to mess it up by sticking too closely to rules."

Sam: "That gives me an idea. Enjoy your bread and thanks for calling. I'll talk to later."

Leslie: "O.k. goodbye… And, uh…, good, luck?" She said awkwardly.

The following day Sam is standing in front of the main entrance for Phizbangs corporate offices, a ten story reflective glass building in the suburbs. He pauses as if to steel himself for what he is about to do.

Inside the guards run interference, but he convinces them to call Mr. Collins secretary and see if he is available for a visit. The secretary is reluctant, but she recognizes the name and against her better judgment, passes the message on. In a moment, Sam is on the elevator, with a couple of security guards who look like former linebackers. The doors close and Sam asks them, "Have you heard of the Barney Doctrine?"

All he gets is a raised eyebrow from the guy to his right.

"Unpleasant things happen in life, but you must never admit it. You must always smile, just like Barney, and if you're your problems don't vanish instantly, all you need to do is sing a song. Now, why don't we sing a song?

When the elevator doors open, the security guards are singing, arm in arm, "I love you. You love me"…Outside of the elevator there is a glass wall, preventing entry to the office. Mr. Collins is standing on the other side, holding up a sheet of paper which reads, "It's good to see you again." Sam begins to speak, but Collins points him to a pad of paper on the floor.

Sam writes: "Sure, under these circumstances. Congratulations on your survival, I mean, success."

Collins writes: "You understand the reason why we had to let you go."

Sam writes: "I understand the real reason and the superficial reason. As well, I understand why you have allowed me into your office today."

Collins writes: "The machine which you built has made Phiz-bang very profitable, but I suspect that you have an understanding of its potential which no one in our research department is capable of."

Sam writes: "Certainly, and I am not surprised, because I know precisely how and why it works. What do you want from me?"

Collins writes: "I think you know. The question is what do you want?

What would make it worth your while to have access to the Replicator 5000?"

Sam writes: "It would be grossly irresponsible of me to reveal what I know about it and the only deal which I am willing to negotiate is one which determines the fate of this company."

Collins writes: "If you use your powers against us, you will never see the machine again. We will sell it to another company for billions and retire in style."

Sam writes: "I might consider bringing down the whole industry, or maybe even convincing the government to take national ownership. You are already too dependent upon our government for research money and market protections."

Collins writes: (In a move of desperation) "I know Bradlebaum."

Sam writes: (Playing dumb) "Who?"

Collins writes: "Dr. David Bradlebaum, the professor of Neuropsychology at I.O. University. He's a good friend of mine. We grew up together and, he told me about your conversation, along with some advice on how to handle you."

Sam writes: "Handle? I doubt that he used that word. He knows little to nothing about this and besides, how could he possibly influence <u>me</u>?"

Collins writes: "He told me that something unexpected has happened to you and that you were upset about it."

Sam writes: (Defensively) "In case you haven't been paying attention to the news lately, I seem to be enjoying my life just fine, thank you, very much."

Collins writes: "Sure, but if you are ever looking for someone whose opinion matters, you could possibly team up together."

Sam writes: "With Bradlebaum? And do what, exactly?"

Collins writes: "Change the world."

Sam writes: "I'm already doing that. Thanks for the advice and goodbye."

Sam hits the button for the lobby, while the security guards are still singing. He walks out and into the sunshine, frustrated by what seemed a very minor victory, not quite sure, but enjoying a vague feeling of expansion. For no particular reason Sam decides to get on a ferry and take a day trip out to Block Island. Warmer weather has moved in, and the impulse for a change of scenery, comes with it.

There is an outcropping of rocks with some trees on the other side of the island from the ferry dock. It is the place where Sam wants to be for the rest of the day. Free from distraction. Free to let his thoughts wander.

He tries to understand what Bradlebaum is up to. What does he think I can do for him? What did he and Collins discuss? Is this some kind of con game? Maybe he should just talk to Bradlebaum and see if he can sniff out some more information.

Hours fly by and there is one more ferry for the day, leaving in about thirty minutes. Sam feels no closer to a solution and doesn't want to go home so after the ferry ride, he decides to wander downtown for some healthy distraction and people watching, or as he likes to call it, "anthropology".

It's Friday night and people are out, having fun, There is enough vicarious joy for Sam to be convinced this was a good idea. As the street lights begin to burn, a vague memory of childhood wonder, at this transition into night, colors his emotions.

On the corner of Third Avenue there is a coffee house with a schedule in the window. A quick glance reveals an open mic poetry slam is taking place. He enters to the sound of these bold words: "The eye within the eye..,

Is swimming in an ocean of language

Forever lost and alive   (Sam does a double take)

Among the Holy contours of life (It's the security guard from Phiz-bang!)

 Following   (Holy sh*t!)

Emblazoned!   (That machine is a
menace)

Without fear or shame!   (Oh, but this is
funny)

Exploring the vision of America   (I
wish Kerouac could be here)

Praising the loneliness

From bleak inhuman architecture

To wild, pure, undisciplined landscape

Pythagorean angels   (Actually,
Kerouac is better off dead)

Exploding into eternity

Under the heavens of belief

With the true burning, supernatural,
madness

Of here and now

Like the peal of a bell

Ringing for the needle..,

That delivers a shot of junk (Puh-
leeeezze)

Turning water into wine

And furniture into character   (Whaa?)

Until the sky begins to speak

The language of geometry."

After a pause, the small audience applauds politely and some of them just snap their fingers. He then steps down and walks toward the tables where most of the finger snappers are to take his seat. A woman in a barrette wraps an arm around him.

Next comes a regular, a man who likes to shout, "The Love Song of J. Alfred Prufrock", with strange enthusiasm. (Eyes, in the audience begin to flutter and roll… "LET US GO THEN.. YOU AND I… WHEN THE EVENING IS SPREAD OUT AGAINST THE SKY… LIKE A PATIENT… ETHERIZED… UPON THE TABLE!…

LET US GO THROUGH CERTAIN HALF DESERTED STREETS, THE MUTTERING RETREATS OF RESTLESS ONE NIGHT CHEAP HOTELS!…

AND SAWDUST RESTAURANTS WITH OYSTER SHELLS!…

STREETS THAT FOLLOW LIKE A TEDIOUS ARGUMENT.. OF INSIDIOUS INTENT!…

TO LEADS YOU TO AN OVERWHELMING QUESTION!

OH, DO NOT ASK, WHAT IS IT?…

LET US GO AND MAKE OUR
VISIT!..."

After a couple of drinks, Sam
decides to throw his hat in the ring. He
gets his name on the list and waits for
about an hour while composing on a
napkin and tapping his feet. When his
turn comes and Sam takes the stage,
there is a noticeable astonishment at the
recognition of his celebrity. Sam
ignores this as if it is an annoyance and
begins:

Prospero has nothing over me...

I laugh at fate and build happy
kingdoms

Where the slaves believe they're free

Where technology is necromance

And the storm I bring is hypnosis

Moving by will and by chance

I engaged for moment in the light

But the burden of existence had no

Guilty pleasure like this fight

Envy the moth, oh, silly human

For they have no lasting desire, but

To burn out yet unproven

Consumption, reproduction, and death

Without the contrivance of capital,

A fate, one could only accept. "

The response from the audience is mild. No one understood that Sam was confessing his moral dilemma. He walks back through the tables and leaves the club. A few people applaud, though it is seems to be sarcastic.

Out in the night air again, Sam smells a food truck up the street. The aromas are too mesmerizing to ignore.

He orders a chicken burrito and heads home, enjoying the warm, savory flavors of Mexico. Tomorrow is another day, he thinks, and has settled on a way to deal with Bradlebaum.

Chapter Eight

In the morning Sam catches the bus which goes directly to the university campus. The sky has more than a few clouds, but at least they are displaying some color; or so it seems from the opposite side of sunglasses. The bus is crowded. He sees what appears to be the only available seat; next to a kid who is reading a Japanese manga comic novel with lurid drawings of a squid-like monster from outer space doing something to a girl in a school uniform. Sam pretends not to notice. He looks for another place to sit, but the bus is packed, so he just stares out the window.

Stepping off of the bus in front of the main building, Sam heads for the psych department. Bradlebaum's office door is open and Sam interrupts the doctor's silence with, "Did Collins inform you to expect me?"

Bradlebaum: "Yes, he did, and let me tell you that he and I are not on the same wavelength when it comes to public policy; if that makes it any easier for you."

Sam: "No, not much…, no."

Bradlebaum: "Sam, you must understand why I am fascinated by what has happened to you; not only from a cultural perspective, but also, and, especially, as a neuro-scientist."

Sam: "So, you told Collins about our conversation and he fired me, because you wanted to get in on it."

Bradlebaum: "I don't think that is exactly what happened. You were all over the news from day one. Don't you think he simply saw the potential and became extremely greedy? ...Look, I know this man, probably better than he knows himself, at least from the viewpoint of motive.

I know that you would probably like to have access to your laboratory so that you can attempt to reverse or control the effects of your condition, despite the upside, and I can help you, but this will be a delicate and somewhat tricky negotiation."

Sam: "The only way this is going to work is by deception."

Bradlebaum: "Precisely."

Sam: "You know he will never forgive you for this."

Bradlebaum: "I have fond memories of him from childhood, but his innocence has evaporated and now he is a pompous ass. Besides that he throws horrible parties with lots of boring self-centered people."

Sam: "Do you have a plan?"

Bradlebaum: "Yes, though it might need some improvement. However, I don't want to tell it here. If you are free, perhaps we could meet for lunch."

Sam: "Time and place?"

Bradlebaum: "That place on Mineola, off of Jericho, at noon."

Sam: "Shakers, I know the place. I'll be looking forward to it."

Bradlebaum: "Good, I will show you my notes and you can show me yours."

Sam: "I think this is moving a bit, too fast."

Bradlebaum: "What do you mean?"

Sam: "Nothing, I'll see you then."

Bradlebaum: "good-bye, Sam"

After a handshake, Sam goes to the library to research con-game techniques. He finds four titles, but two of them are intended for those who work in corrections facilities, one is about Wall Street criminals influencing congress, and the last is about the linguistics of confidence tricks (ideal!).

After some reading Sam heads over to the grill. He is a bit early and Bradlebaum has not arrived yet. He sits in the corner and orders a coffee, pulls out a note pad and scribbles.

Twenty-three minutes later, Mr. B. walks in. Sam rises, respectfully. Mr. B. waves, palm down, for him to sit.

Bradlebaum: "Did you order anything?"

Sam: "Just coffee, I thought I'd wait for you."

Bradlebaum: "That was not necessary, I'm not so..."

Sam: "I know, but my appetite just wasn't ready yet, anyhow."

Bradlebaum: "They have an excellent pastrami sandwich here, which will remain as a pleasant memory for many years to come."

Sam: "That sounds good to me."

Mr. B sits down and says in quiet tone, "Let's not waste time. I am going to set up a meeting with Collins and I will insist that you be there. Naturally, when we begin working, there will be observers, or at least, cameras, and we must be able to convince them that we are not threatened by them... They will be looking for any sign of resistance and while we are concealing we must not appear to conceal. Do you understand?"

Sam: "Certainly, but do you really want to get into the swamps of computer machine codes or do you want to experience a transformation?"

Bradlebaum: (Surprised to receive this offer, unsolicited) "What do you mean?"

The waiter approaches.

Sam: "I'm talking about acquiring abilities which are above and beyond the human condition."

Bradlebaum: (To the waiter) "Two pastrami sandwiches and a pitcher of weiss".

Sam: "I'll have the same… Just kidding, the first order is enough."

Waiter: "Coming right up."

Bradlebaum: "You know that Collins wants to have this… improvement, as well?"

Sam: "Of course I do, but what he doesn't know is that there are side effects."

Bradlebaum: (Slightly concerned) "What are the side effects?"

Sam: "Well... there is obscene wealth and ridiculous fame; that is if you are not too careful (fake chuckling).

Bradlebaum: "But, seriously Sam, didn't you suggest that you were dismayed by some of the effects. I mean, that morning when you first came into my office, you seemed rather... disturbed."

Sam: "That was only because I didn't understand. I wasn't expecting what had happened. The source of my anxiety was merely, confusion. Now, I understand there is an adjustment phase and I have adjusted quite well since then. Don't you agree?"

Bradlebaum: "What do you mean by adjustment?"

Sam: "At first, I didn't have control over it, but over the course of a few days, I learned intuitively, to manage it. And I am convinced that if I could get into that computer, I could shorten that adjustment period. I can't explain it to you here. As I said, there is a lot of coding involved. It would be easier for both of us, if I could just show you. But in order to do that, it is important that only you and maybe Collins are present, though I would prefer, he weren't."

Bradlebaum: "In the lab."

Sam: "Yes, in the lab. Can you set that up?"

Bradlebaum: "I think so, but He is probably going to want to record it."

Sam: "No doubt, but what concerns me, is whether or not he requires a security guard. I am not, at all, comfortable with the possibility that this knowledge could fall into the wrong hands."

Bradlebaum: "I think I could explain it to him in a way that would lower his guard. His real interest is merely, financial power."

Sam: "Yeah, that's my take on him, too... And he's gonna get a boat load of it."

Bradlebaum: "Do you have a preference for when we do this?"

Sam: "I would say.., three days, no two, three is too symbolic. And please, make some kind of suggestion to him that, I just want to make a slight enhancement to what I have accomplished so far. That is my only motivation."

Bradlebaum: "What kind of enhancement?"

Sam: "I want to be able to turn it off completely, at will."

Bradlebaum: "Is that possible?"

Sam: "Yes, I am confident of this... You will see. I can't explain it."

Bradlebaum: "This is going to be good."

Sam: "I hope so."

The waiter brings the provisions, and pours the beer. Sam and Mr. B. toast.

Bradlebaum: "Here is to science."

Sam: "To science."

Bradlebaum: "Oh, hey, I was just wondering… why didn't you attempt to use your powers over Collins?"

Sam: "I couldn't. He had a big glass, soundproof wall where the elevator to his office opened up. We wrote messages to each other. He had a pad of paper on the floor for me."

Bradlebaum: "I'm not surprised. He's seen too many Bond movies. He was obsessed with them as a kid."

Sam: "So, is he the villain?"

Bradlebaum: "Yes, but he believes that he is witty and charming, so that somehow, makes it permissible."

Sam: "It sounds like you are a little eager to burst his bubble."

Bradlebaum: "You are very perceptive."

Later that afternoon, Sam stops by a used bookstore and picks up some hardcover editions of Miss Manners Complete Book of Etiquette and The Adventures of Huckleberry Finn, along with two hardcover copies of, "How to Get People to Do What You Want." Back in his car he is snickering while changing the covers of the first two, with the last two.

Chapter Nine

Roller coasters that go upside-down seven times in a row are not common, but after two and half hours of driving, Sam is riding one, just to release some steam. On his twenty-third boarding, a man wearing a Sponge Bob shirt sits next to him, with a face that is too straight for the shirt. When the coaster begins to jerk into motion, the man turns and says, "Hi, my name Robert Johnson and I work for the CIA."

Sam: "What took you so long?"

Johnson: "Big Government Bureaucracy."

Sam: "Are you being intentionally ironic?"

Johnson: "What?

Sam: "Are you making a joke?"

Johnson: "Yes, of course that was a joke; didn't you think it was funny?"

Sam: "No, what would be funny would be, if you were to say, 'Hi, my name is Robert Johnson, and I have taken on the form of this white guy, to escape from the Devil. Please, just act like you know me, because I think he is in the car right behind us.' "

Johnson: "Oh, the bluuuuueeees guy! (coaster dropped), yeah, I've heard of him."

Sam: (Singing) "I went down to the cross roads… Fell down on my knees!"

Johnson: "I looooovvve that song." (coaster dropped)

Sam: "Of course.., because you wrote it. I mean Robert Johnson wrote it."

Johnson: "Let's get down to business."

Sam: "Can't we just enjoy this ride, Sponge Bob?"

Johnson: "Oh, yeah, sure.., here we go... Wwhheeee!! (Over-acting)."

Sam's cringes with acute social discomfort, then shout's in Dadaist fashion, "Pancakes!!!" (What else could one do in such a situation?)

Johnson: "What??"

Sam: "That's what all the kids are saying these days. They think, 'Wheee', is passé."

Johnson: "Oh..., O.K...., **PANCAKES!!!!!!!**"

The people in the car ahead, turn their heads with puzzled expressions. Sam is amused with himself.

After the ride, Johnson offers Sam a card which reads, "Robert Johnson,

Psy-Ops and Cultural Warfare", with an email address."

Sam: "You're very childlike for someone in such a sober profession."

Johnson: "I think clever would be more accurate. If I wore a black suit and tie with an ear piece; no one would let their guard down around me. Did you have any suspicions?"

Sam: I might just be an outlier but, I wasn't feelin it.

Johnson: "What? You mean my choice of T-shirt?"

Sam: "No, I mean your disposition. You can't just put on a costume and expect that nothing else about you needs to change. You work for an agency that is looking under every rock for bad guys and Sponge-Bob is the eternal optimist, to a fault, that is; he harbors no ill will for any life form. You don't really give off that vibe."

Johnson: "I have eleven years of experience in espionage, seven of which were in hot zones, and you're going to school me?"

Sam: "No, of course not, you would probably kill me and bury me in some third world mass grave, like Dr. Che. Besides, you asked me for my opinion, remember?"

Johnson: "Well, just in case, you feel like serving your country; there is an organization that can facilitate such an endeavor."

Sam: "Do you mean like deposing a legitimately elected official and installing a dictator? ...Sure, sounds like a hoot."

Johnson: "I'm talking about terrorism with a capital T and that rhymes with P and that stands for YOU. Have you seen the terrorist training camps lately? Because I have, and they are advancing their training wwaayy beyond monkey bars and wacky-jacks. Now they are doing head-stands on oil drums and somersaults over barbed wire."

Sam: "I have noooo idea what you are talking about, but I agree with you… That does sound very serious. I wonder who is teaching them how to carry out such sophisticated maneuvers. Golly, if they ever make it to our shores, they might just… I dunno… go into just about any gun store and buy a weapon, no questions asked, and then all that wonderful training will have gone to waste."

Johnson: "Of course, you don't understand this, and I know more about you than you realize, so let me clue you in 'P-man'. The world is hanging in a delicate balance, and the United States is committed to the future…, the future of freedom."

Sam: "What about the future of the planet?"

Johnson: "No, it's pretty much, just about freedom."

Sam: "Thanks for the clarification… Can I go now?"

Johnson: "We are having a meeting at The Pentagon, about you, next Thursday at O' 900 hours. If you are not there, we will be very disappointed."

Sam: "I would be very disappointed if I missed it. I heard you guys can get pretty wild. Can I bring a date?"

Johnson: "No, It's not that kind of function, absolutely not."

Sam: "I have to bring a date. I'll feel naked and alone if I don't have some arm candy."

Johnson: "That is not permissible."

Sam: "What if I bring a guest?"

Johnson: "Guests are not allowed."

Sam: "Who should I bring with me?"

Johnson: "The only people we are interested in are those who have the skills and resources to further the cause of freedom and democracy."

Sam: "That would be my mother. She loves your work, especially the Eisenhower years. And she has a profound understanding of geo-politics… What's the matter agent Johnson, don't you love your mother?"

Johnson: "Of course I love my mother. But, we're talking about the Pentagon, not some game show."

Sam: "You know, there was a study done by the Fischer Institute, and these were corroborated by findings from the Psychiatric Research Council among others, which demonstrated that men who love their mothers are nine times more likely to be successful in life. If you really want me to be successful in my "endeavors" with the Pentagon, then you should have no problem, allowing me to bring my mom."

Johnson: "O.k., o.k., you can bring her, but don't be surprised when General Hitzen insists that she leave."

Sam: "Aren't you, the least bit concerned that I will show up at the Pentagon and stir things up? After all, I just convinced you to allow me to bring my mother and I was just making-up all of that statistical research crap."

Johnson: "I am willing to compromise because I think this could be a great opportunity for you to shape the opinions of the world, maybe even usher in an epoch of world peace."

Sam: "Really? …What's in it for the department of defense?"

Johnson: "Maybe a permanent vacation."

Sam: "Right,… That'll never happen… Have you read General Butler's tract?"

Johnson: "Yeah, 'War Is a Racket', but I'm not sure if I agree with it."

Sam: "Of course not, you're a Pentagon guy. It's you're career! But you cannot deny the fact that a handful of people get rich from wars they do not fight in."

Johnson: "It's too simplistic…, suggesting that the two powers, military and business, are just a global mafia. He ignores the reality of evil forces in the world."

Sam: "Point taken, but his main issue is that, in the end, soldiers pay with their lives or come home with mangled bodies and shattered minds, meanwhile, defense contractors, oil companies, and bankers acquire obscene wealth. How could this seem fair or reasonable to anyone?"

Johnson: "Aren't you the guy who broke up that protest camp at Talinni Park. Remember, the protest against Wall Street? What happened to that guy?"

Sam: "Honestly, I don't remember any of it and there is no way for me to explain why… There always seems to be some kind of stress trigger. I didn't have control over it then, but I have adjusted some, progressively, since then."

Johnson: "So, why are you doing all these media campaigns? Isn't that hypocritical?"

Sam: "It sure looks that way, no doubt. But it should soon make sense."

A vendor walks by...

Sam: "Would you like some cotton candy? It might help with your cover."

Johnson: "Sweet and pink, how could I say no?"

Sam: (Shaking his head) "I don't know what to do with that."

They talk some more and then part ways. In the evening Sam stops by to see Leslie, but she is not exactly pleased to see him.

Leslie: "Even you must know what time it is."

Sam: "I just wanted to tell you that I appreciated what you said to me the other day and that, …well, things are going to change in this little world of ours… in a biiig way."

Leslie: "You mean you're going give up this whole Propagandaman, charade thing?"

Sam: "Just make sure that you take a little time to follow the news over the next couple of weeks."

Leslie: "Are you going after Phiz-bang?"

Sam: "That's just scratching the surface, …you'll see. Anyhow, I'm sorry to have disturbed you. It's just that I'm kind of excited right now. Have a good night." He kisses her and then heads for home.

Chapter Ten

On Thursday morning Sam waltzes
through Pentagon security. His
popularity and charm make the process
seem effortless. Then he strides
through three hallways of Brooks
Brothers and brass.

He arrives at the designated room,
where a man with an ear piece, gives
him a quizzical, up and down look,
then ushers him in. Sam has still no
disturbance of thought, that he is
wearing a silly blue costume; a dime-
store, Halloween version of Superman.
He whispers to the ear-piece guy, "I
don't want them to take me too
seriously."

Inside the meeting hall and full of
bravado, Sam flips his cape as he
addresses the room, "Gentlemen, We
are on the cusp of a new era. The

world is never going to be the same, again."

A four star general interrupts him, "Before you go down a rabbit hole of strategy, let's get one thing clear. Regardless of what agent Johnson told you to get you here, we are not in the business of world peace. All we want is for someone to help us contain the enemy."

Sam: "So …what you really want is a piece of the world and not so much for the world to be at… peace. I get it."

General: "No, that is not it. We do have economic interests which we wish to protect, but we have bigger fish to fry at the moment. We're dealing with loose nukes, chemical weapons, weaponized viruses, terrorism, cyber-warfare, and directed-energy weapons; to name a few.

Sam: "Oh, directed-energy… you mean like, Star Wars, I'm sorry, I mean the Strategic Defense Initiative. I see where this is going. How many of the civilians in this room are defense contractors? Can I just get a show of hands?"

Hesitantly, everyone who is not wearing a uniform raises their hand, except for Johnson. They're seven out of thirteen people.

Sam: (Slipping into a fuzzy - Nicholson impression) "O.k., so you want to move some product, do ya? Well today is your lucky day. I'm sure that you're all a bunch of family loving, patriotic folks. Aren't-chya? But deep down inside, what you really long for is a little scratch from that invisible hand of the free market. And you know what I mean by free? Don't-chya? Yes, of course you do. No limitations whatsoever (his hand filets the air); why should you have to shackle your profits for that old slave driver, Uncle Sam?

General: (Raising his voice) "What the hell is all this supposed to mean?"

Sam: (Raising his voice to match the general's emotion) "What the hell it means General, is that in order to save the free market we must destroy the free market, just like in Vietnam. And I will go on that wall, known as national television, and have a discussion with America about the world that America has created, and all the people who love the American flag so much that they have to put it on everything they own, so they don't forget where they are, will then be ABLE TO HANDLE THE TRUTH!! ...THAT WE ARE MUCH MORE THAN JUST ONE NATION UNDER

GOD, WE ARE ONE PLANET
UNDER THE DOLLAR, WHICH
ALSO HAS THE WORD, "GOD" ON
IT! ...and the word ..."trust". So we
must all trust the dollar and the god for
which it stands. And when I am
finished, I will have proven beyond a
reasonable doubt that America is the
greatest thing that has ever happened
for the cause of freedom and the free
market capitalist individualism of
global corporations, and all that good
stuff!!... Do you catch my... drift,
General, Sir?"

General: "In all honesty,
Propagandaman, we were really just
hoping that you could help the armed
forces make the world safe for
democracy, and maybe help us move
towards more renewable sources of
energy, because it would increase
security at home and abroad. But now

I get the impression that you don't have any interest in such things"

Sam: "Sure, I get it. Let the rest of the world scramble for fossil fuels, while The United States of America moves on, at least militarily, to the future. Have no worries, General. Propagandaman will make it happen. …But, democracy? If by that you mean public participation and influence in the political process, I have to say, isn't that the very definition of socialism? What about the business class, don't they deserve a slice of the pie? After all, they brought the knife."

Admiral: "Perhaps you could at the very least, help write a computer program that would thwart the uranium enrichment programs of rouge nations, the way that stuxnet did. I'm sure that we could fit it into our budget, who's going to notice more defense spending?

. ...Oh, and we'd also like to have something for the kids on our web-site, like the CIA has on theirs. You know, like puzzles and games, ...and maybe a historical quiz."

Sam: "Yeah... I could write you a program, but didn't an eighth grader hack into your system three years ago; oh, I'm sorry, he was a ninth grader. Besides, the kinds of code that I write do not belong in the hands of the government (he makes finger quotes)... unless ... it's a private contractor who works for the government and is therefore a de facto, proxy, extension of the government."

Johnson: "So you'll write the program, if we contract it out to you?"

General #2: (With a Savana accent) "You'll have to forgive Agent Johnson, he's from the state of the dangling chad and they aren't intimately acquainted with sarcasm."

Johnson: "It was a hanging chad and you know that Jeb managed that delicate situation with such nuance it would have made Machiavelli shudder."

Sam: "The way I see it, I was invited here as a consultant, based entirely on the results you have witnessed in the media. If that is what you want, I can deliver it to you, but it can only be on those terms. I have a Sunday morning interview on XYZ's "Meet and Digress." I hope you will tune in, but if you don't, I am sure you will hear about it. In fact, I am sure the whole world will hear about it. Beyond that I believe that we are finished here."

With that, once again, Propagandaman makes his exit.

Chapter Eleven

On Friday afternoon Sam is meeting with Bradlebaum and Collins in the lobby of Phiz-bang. People are staring at him even though he is without the costume. After a quick greeting, the three of them head down to the lab. A fourth man begins to follow and Sam stops walking and simply looks at Bradlebaum. In turn Mr. B looks at Collins, who nods his head towards the fourth man, as if to say, "I told you so". With that, they are three again.

Walking into the lab from the elevator, Sam feels a charge of elation. He powers up the machine, types some codes, and turns to the men who are standing like children anticipating candy. They do not understand what they are witnessing and Sam is uncertain of what he is about to say.

Sam: "In my bag here, I have a copy of Aristotle's, "Organon", the foundation of all logic and critical thinking. These words set the ground rules for determining the difference between truth and falsehood. One could argue that we would not be as advanced as we are without this text. Now I might endure this complicated rhetoric and learn a great many things, but why bother, when I could simply do this…"

He then places the book on the conveyor and presses the button. Two minutes later he receives a pill at the other end and pops it into his mouth.

Collins: "What did you just do?"

Sam: "The machine analyzed the language of the book and converted it to a chemical formula which could be biologically merged with my nervous system. It not only makes learning automatic, but actually infuses the body with understanding. The programs which I have written for this machine do not differentiate between the language of chemistry and other forms of communication. Now, if you are prepared to take the next step, I will offer you the transformation you have eagerly awaited. This is the book which changed my life and I have two, ready to go."

He holds up the two books with the phony jacket facades, titled, "How to get people to do what you want" (actually, "Huckleberry" and "Miss. Manners" are beneath the covers), then feeds them into the machine and waits for his guinea pigs to take the bait. As they place the pills in their mouths, Sam connects a flash drive with a memory scrubbing program to the computer and begins the process of destroying his work; Thus, exacting his revenge on Phiz-bang, Inc.

Two days later, Collins is heading down the Mississippi on a raft with someone he keeps referring to as, "N-word Jim", even though his name is Larry. And Bradlebaum is teaching a handful of students at a community college about the proper way to receive a gift from someone you utterly despise.

Chapter Twelve

Late Sunday morning, on "Meet and Digress", a news talk show that has been falling in the ratings, Propagandaman appears on the screen, looking mischievous. Nevil Dregory is the host. (A musical theme with show identification plays). Times-square is flooded with people watching the giant screens, listening intently, and millions more watch from across the globe.

Nevil: "On today's show we will be speaking with the most talked about man in America, if not the world…, Propagandaman, regarding American exceptionalism and the future of the free market. … Propagandaman, many people are saying that you have really shaken up the world market with your… well as one economist put it, consumer-itis; which he described as, 'a fever that can only be abated by worshiping at the altar of materialism, where the self-appointed Pope Propagandaman proclaims his infallibility, while distorting markets everywhere.'"

P-man: "That's true Nevil; many people are easily influenced by the words and images which are presented to them through mass-media and they don't understand how they are being manipulated. They are led to believe that they are acting in their own best interest, their own happiness, success, glamour, and such things which only feed the ego, but it is a psychological con."

Nevil: "I am surprised to hear you say that. It sounds like the opposite of what you have been promoting. One might ask if you are not a big part of the con."

P-man: "Nevil, the con is a two hundred billion dollar industry; that's a two with eleven zeros behind it. It is true that I have stirred the pot quite well and benefited from it, but now that I have captured everyone's attention I am going to reveal what is really going on. Propaganda is the management of perception. It is to make war the perfect expression of patriotism. It is to make smoking appear cool or sexy. It is to make politicians of all kinds, look like they actually give a crap about those who suffer. It is to make those who are high finance criminals, appear to be philanthropists. It is to claim that moving factories to places where people can be exploited, is economic freedom. It is very simply, public relations. And the term, 'public relations', itself is a massive lie. The truth is that it is manipulation of the masses through language tricks."

Meanwhile the show's producer is losing his mind. "We have to get Nevil to segue into a commercial! Someone go notify the backup guest... And get him to segue to an f-ing commercial!!" The woman who has Nevil's ear says, "I've tried but he's not responding." Nevil has an expression of intense fascination.

P-man: (continuing) "The main problem for the human race is in figuring out which is more important, opinion or truth. If I claim my opinion is more important than truth, then I have given myself permission to believe anything. However, if I claim that truth is more important than my opinion, then I must always be willing to abandon such opinions and those who push them, no matter the consequences."

Back in the control room the producer is getting yelled at through a phone by a network executive. "Ratings don't matter if we have no sponsors! You know what this guy is capable of!!"

Producer: "We are close to a solution now, Sir."

Nevil: So how does one find out what is true?

P-man: "The easiest way is to listen to those who are experts in their fields. Like in a court of law, when they want to know... say, a cause of death. They consult the coroner, not the ice-cream man. That is, unless there was ice-cream at the scene of the crime."

Nevil: "So the next step would be discovering who really is an expert and who is faking it."

P-man: "Yes, exactly, and there are many who get paid very well to fake it... expertise, that is (He winks). The faker is usually the one who acts as if it is not possible for them to ever be mistaken."

Nevil: "Right, as if the position they held must be protected from scrutiny at all costs. ...You know, this may be the one time in the history of this show, that..."

The producer cuts to another talking head in another studio.

Anchor man: "XYZ has just received breaking news out of Miami... Right now, in Miami, Justin Bieber has been arrested on a number of charges. The judge is reading the charges... including resisting arrest, driving under the influence. He's appearing now before the judge for his bond hearing. Let's watch..."

The End

Note: The last four sentences are the words of television journalist, Andrea Mitchell (probably given through her ear-piece).

Appendix

<u>Propaganda Techniques</u>

Edward Filene helped establish the
Institute of Propaganda Analysis in
1937 to educate the American public
about the nature of propaganda and
how to recognize propaganda
techniques. Filene and his colleagues
identified the seven most common
"tricks of the trade" used by successful
propagandists (Marlin 102-106:
Propaganda Critic: Introduction). These
seven techniques are called:

- **Name Calling**

- **Glittering Generalities**

- **Transfer**

- **Testimonial**

- **Plain Folks**

- **Card Stacking**

- **Band Wagon**

- **False Dilemma** (*added*)

These techniques are designed to fool us because the appeal to our emotions rather than to our reason. The techniques identified by the Institute for Propaganda Analysis are further refined by Aaron Delwich in his website, Propaganda where he "discusses various propaganda techniques, provides contemporary examples of their use, and proposes strategies of mental self-defense." By pointing out these techniques, we hope to join with others who have written on this topic to create awareness and encourage serious consideration of the influence of contemporary propaganda directed at us through the various media and suggest ways to guard against its influence on our lives.

Name Calling:

Propagandists use this technique to create fear and arouse prejudice by using negative words (bad names) to create an unfavorable opinion or hatred against a group, beliefs, ideas or institutions they would have us denounce. This method calls for a conclusion without examining the evidence. Name Calling is used as a substitute for arguing the merits of an idea, belief, or proposal. It is often employed using sarcasm and ridicule in political cartoons and writing. When confronted with this technique the Institute for Propaganda Analysis suggests we ask ourselves the following questions: What does the name mean? Is there a real connection between the idea and the name being used? What are the merits of the idea if I leave the name out of consideration?

When examining this technique, try to separate your feelings about the name and the actual idea or proposal (Propaganda Critic: Common Techniques 1).

Glittering Generalities:

Propagandists employ vague, sweeping statements (often slogans or simple catchphrases) using language associated with values and beliefs deeply held by the audience without providing supporting information or reason. They appeal to such notions as honor, glory, love of country, desire for peace, freedom, and family values. The words and phrases are vague and suggest different things to different people but the implication is always favorable. It cannot be proved true or false because it really says little or nothing at all. The Institute of Propaganda Analysis suggests a number of questions we should ask ourselves if we are confronted with this technique: What do the slogans or phrases really mean? Is there a legitimate connection between the idea being discussed and the true meaning of the slogan or phrase being used? What are the merits of the idea itself if it is separated from the slogans or phrases?

Transfer:

Transfer is a technique used to carry over the authority and approval of something we respect and revere to something the propagandist would have us accept. Propagandists often employ symbols (e.g., waving the flag) to stir our emotions and win our approval. The Institute for Propaganda Analysis suggests we ask ourselves these questions when confronted with this technique. What is the speaker trying to pitch? What is the meaning of the thing the propagandist is trying to impart? Is there a legitimate connection between the suggestion made by the propagandist and the person or product? Is there merit in the proposal by itself? When confronted with this technique, question the merits of the idea or proposal independently of the convictions about other persons, ideas, or proposals.

Testimonial:

Propagandists use this technique to associate a respected person or someone with experience to endorse a product or cause by giving it their stamp of approval hoping that the intended audience will follow their example. The Institute for Propaganda Analysis suggests we ask ourselves the following question when confronted with this technique. Who is quoted in the testimonial? Why should we regard this person as an expert or trust their testimony? Is there merit to the idea or product without the testimony? You can guard yourself against this technique by demonstrating that the person giving the testimonial is not a recognized authority, prove they have an agenda or vested interest, or show there is disagreement by other experts.

Plain Folks:

Propagandists use this approach to convince the audience that the spokesperson is from humble origins, someone they can trust and who has their interests at heart. Propagandists have the speaker use ordinary language and mannerisms to reach the audience and identify with their point of view. The Institute for Propaganda Analysis suggests we ask ourselves the following questions before deciding on any issue when confronted with this technique. Is the person credible and trustworthy when they are removed from the situation being discussed? Is the person trying to cover up anything? What are the facts of the situation? When confronted with this type of propaganda consider the ideas and proposals separately from the personality of the presenter.

Bandwagon:

Propagandists use this technique to persuade the audience to follow the crowd. This device creates the impression of widespread support. It reinforces the human desire to be on the winning side. It also plays on feelings of loneliness and isolation. Propagandists use this technique to convince people not already on the bandwagon to join in a mass movement while simultaneously reassuring that those on or partially on should stay aboard. Bandwagon propaganda has taken on a new twist. Propagandists are now trying to convince the target audience that if they don't join in they will be left out. The implication is that if you don't jump on the bandwagon the parade will pass you by. While this is contrary to the other method, it has the same effect: getting the audience to join in with the crowd. The Institute of Propaganda Analysis suggests we ask ourselves the following questions when confronted with this technique. What is the propagandist's program? What is the evidence for and against the program? Even though others are supporting it, why should I? As with most propaganda techniques, getting more information is the best defense. When confronted with Bandwagon propaganda, consider the pros and cons before joining in.

Card Stacking:

Propagandist uses this technique to make the best case possible for his side and the worst for the opposing viewpoint by carefully using only those facts that support his or her side of the argument while attempting to lead the audience into accepting the facts as a conclusion. In other words, the propagandist stacks the cards against the truth. Card stacking is the most difficult technique to detect because it does not provide all of the information necessary for the audience to make an informed decision. The audience must decide what is missing. The Institute for Propaganda Analysis suggests we ask ourselves the following question when confronted with this technique: Are facts being distorted or omitted? What other arguments exist to support these assertions? As with any other propaganda technique, the best defense against Card Stacking is to get as much information that is possible before making a decision.

False dilemma (or dichotomy):

A limited number of options (usually two) are given, while in reality there are more options. A false dilemma is an illegitimate use of the "or" operator. "You're either with us, or against us." Also (false dichotomy): "There are only two kinds of people in this world, those who love pizza or those who hate pizza."

About the author:

Steve is a card carrying member of the human race.

His life has never been the same since he tried ramen noodles at the age of 7.

Sometimes he likes to argue but he never likes to be argumentative.

He used to have a reputation as someone who never wore shoes (except in winter).

Steve has seen a lot of movies and will often bore people with his opinions about them.

He is strangely proud of his ability to consume food that other people don't want.

Steve would never tell you this, but he can play a mean guitar!

He married a girl that he met when he was 3 years old.

Last summer, a 200 lb. tractor wheel fell on his head, but we think he will be alright.

His favorite pastime is walking in the woods.

He knows how to juggle (a bit).

Steve had a dream last night, that Bruce Lee and Michael Jackson became very good friends in heaven. They like to show their moves to one another.

One day, when he grows up, he wants to be a writer.

Made in the USA
Columbia, SC
20 May 2019